Version Management with CVS

for CVS 1.11

Per Cederqvist et al.

A catalogue record for this book is available from the British Library.

First Printing, November 2002 (22/11/2002)

Published by Network Theory Limited.

15 Royal Park
Clifton
Bristol BS8 3AL
United Kingdom

Email: info@network-theory.co.uk

ISBN 0-9541617-1-8

Further information about this book is available from
http://www.network-theory.co.uk/cvs/manual/

Table of Contents

Publisher's Preface 1

1 Overview 3

  1.1 What is CVS? 3

  1.2 What is CVS not? 4

  1.3 A sample session 6

      1.3.1 Getting the source 6

      1.3.2 Committing your changes 7

      1.3.3 Cleaning up 8

      1.3.4 Viewing differences 9

2 The Repository 11

  2.1 Telling CVS where your repository is 11

  2.2 How data is stored in the repository 12

      2.2.1 Where files are stored within the repository .. 12

      2.2.2 File permissions 14

      2.2.3 File Permission issues specific to Windows ... 15

      2.2.4 The attic 16

      2.2.5 The CVS directory in the repository 16

      2.2.6 CVS locks in the repository 17

      2.2.7 How files are stored in the CVSROOT directory 18

  2.3 How data is stored in the working directory 19

  2.4 The administrative files 23

      2.4.1 Editing administrative files 24

  2.5 Multiple repositories 24

  2.6 Creating a repository 25

  2.7 Backing up a repository 25

  2.8 Moving a repository 26

  2.9 Remote repositories 26

      2.9.1 Server requirements 27

      2.9.2 Connecting with rsh 28

      2.9.3 Direct connection with password authentication 29

          2.9.3.1 Setting up the server for password authentication 29

          2.9.3.2 Using the client with password authentication 32

         2.9.3.3 Security considerations with password
                  authentication 33
    2.9.4 Direct connection with GSSAPI 34
    2.9.5 Direct connection with kerberos 34
    2.9.6 Connecting with fork 35
2.10 Read-only repository access 36
2.11 Temporary directories for the server 37

3   Starting a project with CVS 39
3.1 Setting up the files 39
     3.1.1 Creating a directory tree from a number of files
            39
     3.1.2 Creating Files From Other Version Control
            Systems 40
     3.1.3 Creating a directory tree from scratch 41
3.2 Defining the module 41

4   Revisions 43
4.1 Revision numbers 43
4.2 Versions, revisions and releases 43
4.3 Assigning revisions 43
4.4 Tags–Symbolic revisions 44
4.5 Specifying what to tag from the working directory 47
4.6 Specifying what to tag by date or revision 48
4.7 Deleting, moving, and renaming tags 48
4.8 Tagging and adding and removing files 49
4.9 Sticky tags 50

5   Branching and merging 53
5.1 What branches are good for 53
5.2 Creating a branch 53
5.3 Accessing branches 54
5.4 Branches and revisions 55
5.5 Magic branch numbers 56
5.6 Merging an entire branch 57
5.7 Merging from a branch several times 58
5.8 Merging differences between any two revisions 59
5.9 Merging can add or remove files 60
5.10 Merging and keywords 60

6   Recursive behavior 63

7 Adding, removing, and renaming files and directories 65

7.1 Adding files to a directory 65
7.2 Removing files 66
7.3 Removing directories 68
7.4 Moving and renaming files 68
    7.4.1 The Normal way to Rename 69
    7.4.2 Moving the history file 69
    7.4.3 Copying the history file 69
7.5 Moving and renaming directories 70

8 History browsing 73

8.1 Log messages 73
8.2 The history database 73
8.3 User-defined logging 73
8.4 Annotate command 74

9 Handling binary files 75

9.1 The issues with binary files 75
9.2 How to store binary files 76

10 Multiple developers 79

10.1 File status 79
10.2 Bringing a file up to date 81
10.3 Conflicts example 81
10.4 Informing others about commits 84
10.5 Several developers simultaneously attempting to run CVS
    84
10.6 Mechanisms to track who is editing files 85
    10.6.1 Telling CVS to watch certain files 86
    10.6.2 Telling CVS to notify you 86
    10.6.3 How to edit a file which is being watched . . . 88
    10.6.4 Information about who is watching and editing
    89
    10.6.5 Using watches with old versions of CVS 89
10.7 Choosing between reserved or unreserved checkouts . . . 89

11 Revision management 91

11.1 When to commit? 91

12   Keyword substitution 93

12.1	Keyword List	93
12.2	Using keywords	94
12.3	Avoiding substitution	95
12.4	Substitution modes.................................	95
12.5	Problems with the Log keyword.	96

13   Tracking third-party sources 99

13.1	Importing for the first time	99
13.2	Updating with the import command................	100
13.3	Reverting to the latest vendor release...............	100
13.4	How to handle binary files with cvs import..........	101
13.5	How to handle keyword substitution with cvs import	101
13.6	Multiple vendor branches	101

14   How your build system interacts with CVS 103

15   Special Files 105

Appendix A   Guide to CVS commands 107

A.1	Overall structure of CVS commands		107
A.2	CVS's exit status		107
A.3	Default options and the ~/.cvsrc file................		108
A.4	Global options		109
A.5	Common command options.........................		111
A.6	admin—Administration		114
	A.6.1	admin options............................	115
A.7	checkout—Check out sources for editing............		120
	A.7.1	checkout options	121
	A.7.2	checkout examples.......................	123
A.8	commit—Check files into the repository		123
	A.8.1	commit options	124
	A.8.2	commit examples.........................	125
		A.8.2.1 Committing to a branch	125
		A.8.2.2 Creating the branch after editing	125
A.9	diff—Show differences between revisions		126

A.9.1   diff options 126
A.9.2   diff examples............................. 128
A.10   export—Export sources from CVS, similar to checkout
.... 128
A.10.1   export options 129
A.11   history—Show status of files and users 129
A.11.1   history options 130
A.12   import—Import sources into CVS, using vendor branches
.... 132
A.12.1   import options 133
A.12.2   import output 133
A.12.3   import examples 134
A.13   log—Print out log information for files 134
A.13.1   log options............................. 134
A.13.2   log examples 136
A.14   rdiff—'patch' format diffs between releases.......... 136
A.14.1   rdiff options 137
A.14.2   rdiff examples.......................... 137
A.15   release—Indicate that a Module is no longer in use.. 138
A.15.1   release options 138
A.15.2   release output.......................... 139
A.15.3   release examples 139
A.16   update—Bring work tree in sync with repository 140
A.16.1   update options......................... 140
A.16.2   update output 142

Appendix B   Quick reference to CVS commands 145

Appendix C   Reference manual for Administrative files 159
C.1   The modules file.................................... 159
C.1.1   Alias modules 159
C.1.2   Regular modules 160
C.1.3   Ampersand modules 161
C.1.4   Excluding directories 161
C.1.5   Module options 162
C.1.6   How the modules file "program options"
         programs are run.......................... 163
C.2   The cvswrappers file 163
C.3   The commit support files............................ 164
C.3.1   The common syntax 165

C.4   Commitinfo 165
C.5   Verifying log messages 166
C.6   Editinfo.. 167
       C.6.1   Editinfo example 168
C.7   Loginfo 169
       C.7.1   Loginfo example......................... 170
       C.7.2   Keeping a checked out copy 170
C.8   Rcsinfo 170
C.9   Ignoring files via cvsignore 171
C.10   The checkoutlist file 172
C.11   The history file.................................. 173
C.12   Expansions in administrative files 173
C.13   The CVSROOT/config configuration file 174

Appendix D   All environment variables which affect CVS 177

Appendix E   Compatibility between CVS Versions......................... 181

Appendix F   Troubleshooting 183

F.1   Partial list of error messages........................ 183
F.2   Trouble making a connection to a CVS server 190
F.3   Other common problems 191

Appendix G   Credits 193

Appendix H   Dealing with bugs in CVS or this manual....................... 195

Index................................. 197

Publisher's Preface

This manual describes the use of CVS, a version control system.

CVS is *free software*. The term "free software" is sometimes misunderstood — it has nothing to do with price. It is about freedom. It refers to your freedom to run, copy, distribute, study, change and improve the software. With CVS you have all these freedoms.

CVS is part of the GNU Project. The GNU Project was launched in 1984 to develop a complete Unix-like operating system which is free software: the GNU system. It was conceived as a way of bringing back the cooperative spirit that prevailed in the computing community in earlier days. Its goal is to make cooperation possible once again by removing the obstacles to cooperation imposed by the owners of proprietary software. Variants of the GNU operating system, which use the kernel Linux, are now widely used; though these systems are often referred to as "Linux", they are more accurately called GNU/Linux systems.

The Free Software Foundation is a tax-exempt charity that raises funds for work on the GNU Project. It is dedicated to promoting computer users' right to use, study, copy, modify, and redistribute computer programs. You can support the Free Software Foundation by making a donation or ordering manuals, t-shirts and especially CD-ROMs. For more information visit the website **www.gnu.org**.

Brian Gough
Publisher
November 2002

1 Overview

This chapter is for people who have never used CVS, and perhaps have never used version control software before.

If you are already familiar with CVS and are just trying to learn a particular feature or remember a certain command, you can probably skip everything here.

1.1 What is CVS?

CVS is a version control system. Using it, you can record the history of your source files.

For example, bugs sometimes creep in when software is modified, and you might not detect the bug until a long time after you make the modification. With CVS, you can easily retrieve old versions to see exactly which change caused the bug. This can sometimes be a big help.

You could of course save every version of every file you have ever created. This would however waste an enormous amount of disk space. CVS stores all the versions of a file in a single file in a clever way that only stores the differences between versions.

CVS also helps you if you are part of a group of people working on the same project. It is all too easy to overwrite each others' changes unless you are extremely careful. Some editors, like GNU Emacs, try to make sure that the same file is never modified by two people at the same time. Unfortunately, if someone is using another editor, that safeguard will not work. CVS solves this problem by insulating the different developers from each other. Every developer works in his own directory, and CVS merges the work when each developer is done.

CVS started out as a bunch of shell scripts written by Dick Grune, posted to the newsgroup comp.sources.unix in the volume 6 release of December, 1986. While no actual code from these shell scripts is present in the current version of CVS much of the CVS conflict resolution algorithms come from them.

In April, 1989, Brian Berliner designed and coded CVS. Jeff Polk later helped Brian with the design of the CVS module and vendor branch support.

You can get CVS in a variety of ways, including free download from the internet. For more information on downloading CVS and other CVS topics, see:

```
http://www.cvshome.org/
http://www.loria.fr/~molli/cvs-index.html
```

There is a mailing list, known as `info-cvs`, devoted to CVS. To subscribe or unsubscribe write to `info-cvs-request@gnu.org`. If you prefer a usenet group, the right group is `comp.software.config-mgmt` which is for CVS discussions (along with other configuration management systems). In the future, it might be possible to create a `comp.software.config-mgmt.cvs`, but probably only if there is sufficient CVS traffic on `comp.software.config-mgmt`.

You can also subscribe to the bug-cvs mailing list, described in more detail in Appendix H [BUGS], page 195. To subscribe send mail to bug-cvs-request@gnu.org.

1.2 What is CVS not?

CVS can do a lot of things for you, but it does not try to be everything for everyone.

CVS is not a build system.

> Though the structure of your repository and modules file interact with your build system (e.g. 'Makefile's), they are essentially independent.

> CVS does not dictate how you build anything. It merely stores files for retrieval in a tree structure you devise.

> CVS does not dictate how to use disk space in the checked out working directories. If you write your 'Makefile's or scripts in every directory so they have to know the relative positions of everything else, you wind up requiring the entire repository to be checked out.

> If you modularize your work, and construct a build system that will share files (via links, mounts, VPATH in 'Makefile's, etc.), you can arrange your disk usage however you like.

> But you have to remember that *any* such system is a lot of work to construct and maintain. CVS does not address the issues involved.

> Of course, you should place the tools created to support such a build system (scripts, 'Makefile's, etc) under CVS.

> Figuring out what files need to be rebuilt when something changes is, again, something to be handled outside the scope of CVS. One traditional approach is to use **make** for building, and use some automated tool for generating the dependencies which **make** uses.

> See Chapter 14 [Builds], page 103, for more information on doing builds in conjunction with CVS.

CVS is not a substitute for management.

> Your managers and project leaders are expected to talk to you frequently enough to make certain you are aware of schedules, merge points, branch names and release dates. If they don't, CVS can't help.
>
> CVS is an instrument for making sources dance to your tune. But you are the piper and the composer. No instrument plays itself or writes its own music.

CVS is not a substitute for developer communication.

> When faced with conflicts within a single file, most developers manage to resolve them without too much effort. But a more general definition of "conflict" includes problems too difficult to solve without communication between developers.
>
> CVS cannot determine when simultaneous changes within a single file, or across a whole collection of files, will logically conflict with one another. Its concept of a *conflict* is purely textual, arising when two changes to the same base file are near enough to spook the merge (i.e. diff3) command.
>
> CVS does not claim to help at all in figuring out non-textual or distributed conflicts in program logic.
>
> For example: Say you change the arguments to function X defined in file 'A'. At the same time, someone edits file 'B', adding new calls to function X using the old arguments. You are outside the realm of CVS's competence.
>
> Acquire the habit of reading specs and talking to your peers.

CVS does not have change control

> Change control refers to a number of things. First of all it can mean *bug-tracking*, that is being able to keep a database of reported bugs and the status of each one (is it fixed? in what release? has the bug submitter agreed that it is fixed?). For interfacing CVS to an external bug-tracking system, see the 'rcsinfo' and 'verifymsg' files (see Appendix C [Administrative files], page 159).
>
> Another aspect of change control is keeping track of the fact that changes to several files were in fact changed together as one logical change. If you check in several files in a single cvs commit operation, CVS then forgets that those files were checked in together, and the fact that they have the same log message is the only thing tying them together. Keeping a GNU style 'ChangeLog' can help somewhat.

Another aspect of change control, in some systems, is the ability to keep track of the status of each change. Some changes have been written by a developer, others have been reviewed by a second developer, and so on. Generally, the way to do this with CVS is to generate a diff (using `cvs diff` or `diff`) and email it to someone who can then apply it using the `patch` utility. This is very flexible, but depends on mechanisms outside CVS to make sure nothing falls through the cracks.

CVS is not an automated testing program

It should be possible to enforce mandatory use of a test-suite using the `commitinfo` file. I haven't heard a lot about projects trying to do that or whether there are subtle gotchas, however.

CVS does not have a builtin process model

Some systems provide ways to ensure that changes or releases go through various steps, with various approvals as needed. Generally, one can accomplish this with CVS but it might be a little more work. In some cases you'll want to use the 'commitinfo', 'loginfo', 'rcsinfo', or 'verifymsg' files, to require that certain steps be performed before cvs will allow a checkin. Also consider whether features such as branches and tags can be used to perform tasks such as doing work in a development tree and then merging certain changes over to a stable tree only once they have been proven.

1.3 A sample session

As a way of introducing CVS, we'll go through a typical work-session using CVS. The first thing to understand is that CVS stores all files in a centralized *repository* (see Chapter 2 [Repository], page 11); this section assumes that a repository is set up.

Suppose you are working on a simple compiler. The source consists of a handful of C files and a 'Makefile'. The compiler is called 'tc' (Trivial Compiler), and the repository is set up so that there is a module called 'tc'.

1.3.1 Getting the source

The first thing you must do is to get your own working copy of the source for 'tc'. For this, you use the `checkout` command:

```
$ cvs checkout tc
```

This will create a new directory called 'tc' and populate it with the source files.

```
$ cd tc
$ ls
CVS  Makefile  backend.c  driver.c  frontend.c  parser.c
```

The 'CVS' directory is used internally by CVS. Normally, you should not modify or remove any of the files in it.

You start your favorite editor, hack away at 'backend.c', and a couple of hours later you have added an optimization pass to the compiler. A note to RCS and SCCS users: There is no need to lock the files that you want to edit. See Chapter 10 [Multiple developers], page 79, for an explanation.

1.3.2 Committing your changes

When you have checked that the compiler is still compilable you decide to make a new version of 'backend.c'. This will store your new 'backend.c' in the repository and make it available to anyone else who is using that same repository.

```
$ cvs commit backend.c
```

CVS starts an editor, to allow you to enter a log message. You type in "Added an optimization pass.", save the temporary file, and exit the editor.

The environment variable $CVSEDITOR determines which editor is started. If $CVSEDITOR is not set, then if the environment variable $EDITOR is set, it will be used. If both $CVSEDITOR and $EDITOR are not set then there is a default which will vary with your operating system, for example vi for unix or notepad for Windows NT/95.

In addition, CVS checks the $VISUAL environment variable. Opinions vary on whether this behavior is desirable and whether future releases of CVS should check $VISUAL or ignore it. You will be OK either way if you make sure that $VISUAL is either unset or set to the same thing as $EDITOR.

When CVS starts the editor, it includes a list of files which are modified. For the CVS client, this list is based on comparing the modification time of the file against the modification time that the file had when it was last gotten or updated. Therefore, if a file's modification time has changed but its contents have not, it will show up as modified. The simplest way to handle this is simply not to worry about it—if you proceed with the commit CVS will detect that the contents are not modified and treat it as an unmodified file. The next update will clue CVS in to the fact that the file is unmodified, and it will reset its stored timestamp so that the file will not show up in future editor sessions.

If you want to avoid starting an editor you can specify the log message on the command line using the '-m' flag instead, like this:

```
$ cvs commit -m "Added an optimization pass" backend.c
```

1.3.3 Cleaning up

Before you turn to other tasks you decide to remove your working copy of tc. One acceptable way to do that is of course

```
$ cd ..
$ rm -r tc
```

but a better way is to use the **release** command (see Section A.15 [release], page 138):

```
$ cd ..
$ cvs release -d tc
M driver.c
? tc
You have [1] altered files in this repository.
Are you sure you want to release (and delete)
directory 'tc': n
** 'release' aborted by user choice.
```

The **release** command checks that all your modifications have been committed. If history logging is enabled it also makes a note in the history file. See Section C.11 [history file], page 173.

When you use the '-d' flag with **release**, it also removes your working copy.

In the example above, the **release** command wrote a couple of lines of output. '? tc' means that the file 'tc' is unknown to CVS. That is nothing to worry about: 'tc' is the executable compiler, and it should not be stored in the repository. See Section C.9 [cvsignore], page 171, for information about how to make that warning go away. See Section A.15.2 [release output], page 139, for a complete explanation of all possible output from **release**.

'M driver.c' is more serious. It means that the file 'driver.c' has been modified since it was checked out.

The **release** command always finishes by telling you how many modified files you have in your working copy of the sources, and then asks you for confirmation before deleting any files or making any note in the history file.

You decide to play it safe and answer *n* (RET) when **release** asks for confirmation.

1.3.4 Viewing differences

You do not remember modifying 'driver.c', so you want to see what has happened to that file.

```
$ cd tc
$ cvs diff driver.c
```

This command runs diff to compare the version of 'driver.c' that you checked out with your working copy. When you see the output you remember that you added a command line option that enabled the optimization pass. You check it in, and release the module.

```
$ cvs commit -m "Added an optimization pass" driver.c
Checking in driver.c;
/usr/local/cvsroot/tc/driver.c,v  <--  driver.c
new revision: 1.2; previous revision: 1.1
done
$ cd ..
$ cvs release -d tc
? tc
You have [0] altered files in this repository.
Are you sure you want to release (and delete)
directory 'tc': y
```

2 The Repository

The CVS *repository* stores a complete copy of all the files and directories which are under version control.

Normally, you never access any of the files in the repository directly. Instead, you use CVS commands to get your own copy of the files into a *working directory*, and then work on that copy. When you've finished a set of changes, you check (or *commit*) them back into the repository. The repository then contains the changes which you have made, as well as recording exactly what you changed, when you changed it, and other such information. Note that the repository is not a subdirectory of the working directory, or vice versa; they should be in separate locations.

CVS can access a repository by a variety of means. It might be on the local computer, or it might be on a computer across the room or across the world. To distinguish various ways to access a repository, the repository name can start with an *access method*. For example, the access method `:local:` means to access a repository directory, so the repository `:local:/usr/local/cvsroot` means that the repository is in '`/usr/local/cvsroot`' on the computer running CVS. For information on other access methods, see Section 2.9 [Remote repositories], page 26.

If the access method is omitted, then if the repository does not contain '`:`', then `:local:` is assumed. If it does contain '`:`' then either `:ext:` or `:server:` is assumed. For example, if you have a local repository in '`/usr/local/cvsroot`', you can use `/usr/local/cvsroot` instead of `:local:/usr/local/cvsroot`. But if (under Windows NT, for example) your local repository is '`c:\src\cvsroot`', then you must specify the access method, as in `:local:c:\src\cvsroot`.

The repository is split in two parts. '`$CVSROOT/CVSROOT`' contains administrative files for CVS. The other directories contain the actual user-defined modules.

2.1 Telling CVS where your repository is

There are several ways to tell CVS where to find the repository. You can name the repository on the command line explicitly, with the `-d` (for "directory") option:

```
cvs -d /usr/local/cvsroot checkout yoyodyne/tc
```

Or you can set the `$CVSROOT` environment variable to an absolute path to the root of the repository, '`/usr/local/cvsroot`' in this example. To set `$CVSROOT`, csh and `tcsh` users should have this line in their '`.cshrc`' or '`.tcshrc`' files:

```
setenv CVSROOT /usr/local/cvsroot
```

sh and bash users should instead have these lines in their '.profile' or
'.bashrc':

```
CVSROOT=/usr/local/cvsroot
export CVSROOT
```

A repository specified with -d will override the $CVSROOT environment
variable. Once you've checked a working copy out from the repository, it
will remember where its repository is (the information is recorded in the
'CVS/Root' file in the working copy).

The -d option and the 'CVS/Root' file both override the $CVSROOT envi-
ronment variable. If -d option differs from 'CVS/Root', the former is used.
Of course, for proper operation they should be two ways of referring to
the same repository.

2.2 How data is stored in the repository

For most purposes it isn't important *how* CVS stores information in the
repository. In fact, the format has changed in the past, and is likely to
change in the future. Since in almost all cases one accesses the repository
via CVS commands, such changes need not be disruptive.

However, in some cases it may be necessary to understand how CVS stores
data in the repository, for example you might need to track down CVS
locks (see Section 10.5 [Concurrency], page 84) or you might need to deal
with the file permissions appropriate for the repository.

2.2.1 Where files are stored within the repository

The overall structure of the repository is a directory tree corresponding
to the directories in the working directory. For example, supposing the
repository is in

```
/usr/local/cvsroot
```

here is a possible directory tree (showing only the directories):

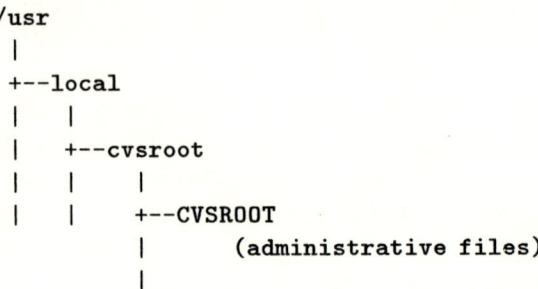

```
/usr
  |
  +--local
  |   |
  |   +--cvsroot
  |   |   |
  |   |   +--CVSROOT
  |           (administrative files)
  |
```

```
          +--gnu
          |    |
          |    +--diff
          |    |    (source code to GNU diff)
          |    |
          |    +--rcs
          |    |    (source code to RCS)
          |    |
          |    +--cvs
          |         (source code to CVS)
          |
          +--yoyodyne
               |
               +--tc
               |    |
               |    +--man
               |    |
               |    +--testing
               |
               +--(other Yoyodyne software)
```

With the directories are *history files* for each file under version control.
The name of the history file is the name of the corresponding file with ',v'
appended to the end. Here is what the repository for the 'yoyodyne/tc'
directory might look like:

```
$CVSROOT
   |
   +--yoyodyne
   |    |
   |    +--tc
   |    |    |
   |         +--Makefile,v
   |         +--backend.c,v
   |         +--driver.c,v
   |         +--frontend.c,v
   |         +--parser.c,v
   |         +--man
   |         |    |
   |         |    +--tc.1,v
   |         |
   |         +--testing
   |              |
```

```
+--testpgm.t,v
+--test2.t,v
```

The history files contain, among other things, enough information to recreate any revision of the file, a log of all commit messages and the user-name of the person who committed the revision. The history files are known as *RCS files*, because the first program to store files in that format was a version control system known as RCS. For a full description of the file format, see the man page *rcsfile(5)*, distributed with RCS, or the file 'doc/RCSFILES' in the CVS source distribution. This file format has become very common—many systems other than CVS or RCS can at least import history files in this format.

The RCS files used in CVS differ in a few ways from the standard format. The biggest difference is magic branches; for more information see Section 5.5 [Magic branch numbers], page 56. Also in CVS the valid tag names are a subset of what RCS accepts; for CVS's rules see Section 4.4 [Tags], page 44.

2.2.2 File permissions

All ',v' files are created read-only, and you should not change the permission of those files. The directories inside the repository should be writable by the persons that have permission to modify the files in each directory. This normally means that you must create a UNIX group (see group(5)) consisting of the persons that are to edit the files in a project, and set up the repository so that it is that group that owns the directory.

This means that you can only control access to files on a per-directory basis.

Note that users must also have write access to check out files, because CVS needs to create lock files (see Section 10.5 [Concurrency], page 84).

Also note that users must have write access to the 'CVSROOT/val-tags' file. CVS uses it to keep track of what tags are valid tag names (it is sometimes updated when tags are used, as well as when they are created).

Each RCS file will be owned by the user who last checked it in. This has little significance; what really matters is who owns the directories.

CVS tries to set up reasonable file permissions for new directories that are added inside the tree, but you must fix the permissions manually when a new directory should have different permissions than its parent directory. If you set the CVSUMASK environment variable that will control the file permissions which CVS uses in creating directories and/or files in the repository. CVSUMASK does not affect the file permissions in the working directory; such files have the permissions which are typical for newly created files, except that sometimes CVS creates them read-only (see the sections on watches, Section 10.6.1 [Setting a watch], page 86; -r, Section A.4 [Global options], page 109; or CVSREAD, Appendix D [Environment variables], page 177).

Note that using the client/server CVS (see Section 2.9 [Remote repositories], page 26), there is no good way to set CVSUMASK; the setting on the client machine has no effect. If you are connecting with rsh or ssh, you can set CVSUMASK in '.bashrc' or '.cshrc', as described in the documentation for your operating system. This behavior might change in future versions of CVS; do not rely on the setting of CVSUMASK on the client having no effect.

Using pserver, you will generally need stricter permissions on the CVS-ROOT directory and directories above it in the tree; see Section 2.9.3.3 [Password authentication security], page 33.

Some operating systems have features which allow a particular program to run with the ability to perform operations which the caller of the program could not. For example, the set user ID (setuid) or set group ID (setgid) features of unix or the installed image feature of VMS. CVS was not written to use such features and therefore attempting to install CVS in this fashion will provide protection against only accidental lapses; anyone who is trying to circumvent the measure will be able to do so, and depending on how you have set it up may gain access to more than just CVS. You may wish to instead consider pserver. It shares some of the same attributes, in terms of possibly providing a false sense of security or opening security holes wider than the ones you are trying to fix, so read the documentation on pserver security carefully if you are considering this option (Section 2.9.3.3 [Password authentication security], page 33).

2.2.3 File Permission issues specific to Windows

Some file permission issues are specific to Windows operating systems (Windows 95, Windows NT, and presumably future operating systems in this family. Some of the following might apply to OS/2 but I'm not sure).

If you are using local CVS and the repository is on a networked file system which is served by the Samba SMB server, some people have reported problems with permissions. Enabling WRITE=YES in the samba configuration is said to fix/workaround it. Disclaimer: I haven't investigated enough to know the implications of enabling that option, nor do I know whether there is something which CVS could be doing differently in order to avoid the problem. If you find something out, please let us know as described in Appendix H [BUGS], page 195.

2.2.4 The attic

You will notice that sometimes CVS stores an RCS file in the `Attic`. For example, if the CVSROOT is '/usr/local/cvsroot' and we are talking about the file 'backend.c' in the directory 'yoyodyne/tc', then the file normally would be in

    /usr/local/cvsroot/yoyodyne/tc/backend.c,v

but if it goes in the attic, it would be in

    /usr/local/cvsroot/yoyodyne/tc/Attic/backend.c,v

instead. It should not matter from a user point of view whether a file is in the attic; CVS keeps track of this and looks in the attic when it needs to. But in case you want to know, the rule is that the RCS file is stored in the attic if and only if the head revision on the trunk has state **dead**. A **dead** state means that file has been removed, or never added, for that revision. For example, if you add a file on a branch, it will have a trunk revision in **dead** state, and a branch revision in a non-**dead** state.

2.2.5 The CVS directory in the repository

The 'CVS' directory in each repository directory contains information such as file attributes (in a file called 'CVS/fileattr'. In the future additional files may be added to this directory, so implementations should silently ignore additional files.

This behavior is implemented only by CVS 1.7 and later; for details see Section 10.6.5 [Watches Compatibility], page 89.

The format of the fileattr file is a series of entries of the following form (where '{' and '}' means the text between the braces can be repeated zero or more times):

ent-type filename <tab> *attrname* = *attrval* {; *attrname* = *attrval*} <linefeed>

ent-type is 'F' for a file, in which case the entry specifies the attributes for that file.

ent-type is 'D', and *filename* empty, to specify default attributes to be used for newly added files.

Other *ent-type* are reserved for future expansion. CVS 1.9 and older will delete them any time it writes file attributes. CVS 1.10 and later will preserve them.

Note that the order of the lines is not significant; a program writing the fileattr file may rearrange them at its convenience.

There is currently no way of quoting tabs or linefeeds in the filename, '=' in *attrname*, ';' in *attrval*, etc. Note: some implementations also don't handle a NUL character in any of the fields, but implementations are encouraged to allow it.

By convention, *attrname* starting with '_' is for an attribute given special meaning by CVS; other *attrnames* are for user-defined attributes (or will be, once implementations start supporting user-defined attributes).

Builtin attributes:

_watched   Present means the file is watched and should be checked out read-only.

_watchers   Users with watches for this file. Value is *watcher* > *type* { , *watcher* > *type* } where *watcher* is a username, and *type* is zero or more of edit,unedit,commit separated by '+' (that is, nothing if none; there is no "none" or "all" keyword).

_editors   Users editing this file. Value is *editor* > *val* { , *editor* > *val* } where *editor* is a username, and *val* is *time+hostname+pathname*, where *time* is when the cvs edit command (or equivalent) happened, and *hostname* and *pathname* are for the working directory.

Example:

```
Ffile1 _watched=;_watchers=joe>edit,mary>commit
Ffile2 _watched=;_editors=sue>8 Jan 1975+workstn1+/home/sue/cvs
D _watched=
```

means that the file 'file1' should be checked out read-only. Furthermore, joe is watching for edits and mary is watching for commits. The file 'file2' should be checked out read-only; sue started editing it on 8 Jan 1975 in the directory '/home/sue/cvs' on the machine workstn1. Future files which are added should be checked out read-only. To represent this example here, we have shown a space after 'D', 'Ffile1', and 'Ffile2', but in fact there must be a single tab character there and no spaces.

2.2.6 CVS locks in the repository

For an introduction to CVS locks focusing on user-visible behavior, see Section 10.5 [Concurrency], page 84. The following section is aimed at people who are writing tools which want to access a CVS repository without interfering with other tools acessing the same repository. If you find yourself confused by concepts described here, like *read lock*, *write lock*, and *deadlock*, you might consult the literature on operating systems or databases.

Any file in the repository with a name starting with '#cvs.rfl.' is a read lock. Any file in the repository with a name starting with '#cvs.wfl' is a write lock. Old versions of CVS (before CVS 1.5) also created files with names starting with '#cvs.tfl', but they are not discussed here. The directory '#cvs.lock' serves as a master lock. That is, one must obtain this lock first before creating any of the other locks.

To obtain a readlock, first create the '#cvs.lock' directory. This operation must be atomic (which should be true for creating a directory under most operating systems). If it fails because the directory already existed, wait for a while and try again. After obtaining the '#cvs.lock' lock, create a file whose name is '#cvs.rfl.' followed by information of your choice (for example, hostname and process identification number). Then remove the '#cvs.lock' directory to release the master lock. Then proceed with reading the repository. When you are done, remove the '#cvs.rfl' file to release the read lock.

To obtain a writelock, first create the '#cvs.lock' directory, as with a readlock. Then check that there are no files whose names start with '#cvs.rfl.'. If there are, remove '#cvs.lock', wait for a while, and try again. If there are no readers, then create a file whose name is '#cvs.wfl' followed by information of your choice (for example, hostname and process identification number). Hang on to the '#cvs.lock' lock. Proceed with writing the repository. When you are done, first remove the '#cvs.wfl' file and then the '#cvs.lock' directory. Note that unlike the '#cvs.rfl' file, the '#cvs.wfl' file is just informational; it has no effect on the locking operation beyond what is provided by holding on to the '#cvs.lock' lock itself.

Note that each lock (writelock or readlock) only locks a single directory in the repository, including 'Attic' and 'CVS' but not including subdirectories which represent other directories under version control. To lock an entire tree, you need to lock each directory (note that if you fail to obtain any lock you need, you must release the whole tree before waiting and trying again, to avoid deadlocks).

Note also that CVS expects writelocks to control access to individual 'foo,v' files. RCS has a scheme where the ',foo,' file serves as a lock, but CVS does not implement it and so taking out a CVS writelock is recommended. See the comments at rcs_internal_lockfile in the CVS source code for further discussion/rationale.

2.2.7 How files are stored in the CVSROOT directory

The '$CVSROOT/CVSROOT' directory contains the various administrative files. In some ways this directory is just like any other directory in the repository; it contains RCS files whose names end in ',v', and many of the CVS commands operate on it the same way. However, there are a few differences.

For each administrative file, in addition to the RCS file, there is also a
checked out copy of the file. For example, there is an RCS file 'loginfo,v'
and a file 'loginfo' which contains the latest revision contained in
'loginfo,v'. When you check in an administrative file, CVS should print

> cvs commit: Rebuilding administrative file database

and update the checked out copy in '$CVSROOT/CVSROOT'. If it does not,
there is something wrong (see Appendix H [BUGS], page 195). To add
your own files to the files to be updated in this fashion, you can add them
to the 'checkoutlist' administrative file (see Section C.10 [checkoutlist],
page 172).

By default, the 'modules' file behaves as described above. If the modules
file is very large, storing it as a flat text file may make looking up modules
slow (I'm not sure whether this is as much of a concern now as when
CVS first evolved this feature; I haven't seen benchmarks). Therefore, by
making appropriate edits to the CVS source code one can store the modules
file in a database which implements the ndbm interface, such as Berkeley
db or GDBM. If this option is in use, then the modules database will be
stored in the files 'modules.db', 'modules.pag', and/or 'modules.dir'.

For information on the meaning of the various administrative files, see
Appendix C [Administrative files], page 159.

2.3 How data is stored in the working directory

While we are discussing CVS internals which may become visible from
time to time, we might as well talk about what CVS puts in the 'CVS'
directories in the working directories. As with the repository, CVS handles
this information and one can usually access it via CVS commands. But
in some cases it may be useful to look at it, and other programs, such as
the jCVS graphical user interface or the VC package for emacs, may need
to look at it. Such programs should follow the recommendations in this
section if they hope to be able to work with other programs which use
those files, including future versions of the programs just mentioned and
the command-line CVS client.

The 'CVS' directory contains several files. Programs which are reading
this directory should silently ignore files which are in the directory but
which are not documented here, to allow for future expansion.

The files are stored according to the text file convention for the system in
question. This means that working directories are not portable between
systems with differing conventions for storing text files. This is intentional,
on the theory that the files being managed by CVS probably will not be
portable between such systems either.

'Root'   This file contains the current CVS root, as described in Section 2.1 [Specifying a repository], page 11.

'Repository'

This file contains the directory within the repository which the current directory corresponds with. It can be either an absolute pathname or a relative pathname; CVS has had the ability to read either format since at least version 1.3 or so. The relative pathname is relative to the root, and is the more sensible approach, but the absolute pathname is quite common and implementations should accept either. For example, after the command

```
cvs -d :local:/usr/local/cvsroot
    checkout yoyodyne/tc
```

'Root' will contain

```
:local:/usr/local/cvsroot
```

and 'Repository' will contain either

```
/usr/local/cvsroot/yoyodyne/tc
```

or

```
yoyodyne/tc
```

If the particular working directory does not correspond to a directory in the repository, then 'Repository' should contain 'CVSROOT/Emptydir'.

'Entries'   This file lists the files and directories in the working directory. The first character of each line indicates what sort of line it is. If the character is unrecognized, programs reading the file should silently skip that line, to allow for future expansion.

If the first character is '/', then the format is:

/name/revision/timestamp[+conflict]/options/tagdate

where '[' and ']' are not part of the entry, but instead indicate that the '+' and conflict marker are optional. name is the name of the file within the directory. revision is the revision that the file in the working derives from, or '0' for an added file, or '−' followed by a revision for a removed file. timestamp is the timestamp of the file at the time that CVS created it; if the timestamp differs with the actual modification time of the file it means the file has been modified. It is stored in the format used by the ISO C asctime() function (for example, 'Sun Apr 7 01:29:26 1996'). One may write a string which is not in that format, for example, 'Result of

merge', to indicate that the file should always be considered
to be modified. This is not a special case; to see whether a
file is modified a program should take the timestamp of the
file and simply do a string compare with *timestamp*. If there
was a conflict, *conflict* can be set to the modification time
of the file after the file has been written with conflict markers (see Section 10.3 [Conflicts example], page 81). Thus
if *conflict* is subsequently the same as the actual modification time of the file it means that the user has obviously not
resolved the conflict. *options* contains sticky options (for example '-kb' for a binary file). *tagdate* contains 'T' followed
by a tag name, or 'D' for a date, followed by a sticky tag or
date. Note that if *timestamp* contains a pair of timestamps
separated by a space, rather than a single timestamp, you
are dealing with a version of CVS earlier than CVS 1.5 (not
documented here).

The timezone on the timestamp in CVS/Entries (local or
universal) should be the same as the operating system stores
for the timestamp of the file itself. For example, on Unix the
file's timestamp is in universal time (UT), so the timestamp
in CVS/Entries should be too. On VMS, the file's timestamp
is in local time, so CVS on VMS should use local time. This
rule is so that files do not appear to be modified merely because the timezone changed (for example, to or from summer
time).

If the first character of a line in 'Entries' is 'D', then it indicates a subdirectory. 'D' on a line all by itself indicates that
the program which wrote the 'Entries' file does record subdirectories (therefore, if there is such a line and no other lines
beginning with 'D', one knows there are no subdirectories).
Otherwise, the line looks like:

   D/ *name* / *filler1* / *filler2* / *filler3* / *filler4*

where *name* is the name of the subdirectory, and all the
filler fields should be silently ignored, for future expansion.
Programs which modify Entries files should preserve these
fields.

The lines in the 'Entries' file can be in any order.

'Entries.Log'

   This file does not record any information beyond that in
   'Entries', but it does provide a way to update the information without having to rewrite the entire 'Entries'
   file, including the ability to preserve the information even if

the program writing 'Entries' and 'Entries.Log' abruptly aborts. Programs which are reading the 'Entries' file should also check for 'Entries.Log'. If the latter exists, they should read 'Entries' and then apply the changes mentioned in 'Entries.Log'. After applying the changes, the recommended practice is to rewrite 'Entries' and then delete 'Entries.Log'. The format of a line in 'Entries.Log' is a single character command followed by a space followed by a line in the format specified for a line in 'Entries'. The single character command is 'A' to indicate that the entry is being added, 'R' to indicate that the entry is being removed, or any other character to indicate that the entire line in 'Entries.Log' should be silently ignored (for future expansion). If the second character of the line in 'Entries.Log' is not a space, then it was written by an older version of CVS (not documented here).

Programs which are writing rather than reading can safely ignore 'Entries.Log' if they so choose.

'Entries.Backup'

This is a temporary file. Recommended usage is to write a new entries file to 'Entries.Backup', and then to rename it (atomically, where possible) to 'Entries'.

'Entries.Static'

The only relevant thing about this file is whether it exists or not. If it exists, then it means that only part of a directory was gotten and CVS will not create additional files in that directory. To clear it, use the **update** command with the '-d' option, which will get the additional files and remove 'Entries.Static'.

'Tag'   This file contains per-directory sticky tags or dates. The first character is 'T' for a branch tag, 'N' for a non-branch tag, or 'D' for a date, or another character to mean the file should be silently ignored, for future expansion. This character is followed by the tag or date. Note that per-directory sticky tags or dates are used for things like applying to files which are newly added; they might not be the same as the sticky tags or dates on individual files. For general information on sticky tags and dates, see Section 4.9 [Sticky tags], page 50.

'Checkin.prog'
'Update.prog'

These files store the programs specified by the '-i' and '-u' options in the modules file, respectively.

'Notify'   This file stores notifications (for example, for edit or
                unedit) which have not yet been sent to the server. Its
                format is not yet documented here.

'Notify.tmp'
                This file is to 'Notify' as 'Entries.Backup' is to 'Entries'.
                That is, to write 'Notify', first write the new contents to
                'Notify.tmp' and then (atomically where possible), rename
                it to 'Notify'.

'Base'   If watches are in use, then an edit command stores the orig-
                inal copy of the file in the 'Base' directory. This allows the
                unedit command to operate even if it is unable to commu-
                nicate with the server.

'Baserev'   The file lists the revision for each of the files in the 'Base'
                directory. The format is:

                        Bname/rev/expansion

                where *expansion* should be ignored, to allow for future ex-
                pansion.

'Baserev.tmp'
                This file is to 'Baserev' as 'Entries.Backup' is to 'Entries'.
                That is, to write 'Baserev', first write the new contents to
                'Baserev.tmp' and then (atomically where possible), rename
                it to 'Baserev'.

'Template'   This file contains the template specified by the 'rcsinfo' file
                (see Section C.8 [rcsinfo], page 170). It is only used by the
                client; the non-client/server CVS consults 'rcsinfo' directly.

2.4 The administrative files

The directory '$CVSROOT/CVSROOT' contains some *administrative files*. See
Appendix C [Administrative files], page 159, for a complete description.
You can use CVS without any of these files, but some commands work
better when at least the 'modules' file is properly set up.

The most important of these files is the 'modules' file. It defines all
modules in the repository. This is a sample 'modules' file.

```
CVSROOT         CVSROOT
modules         CVSROOT modules
cvs             gnu/cvs
rcs             gnu/rcs
diff            gnu/diff
tc              yoyodyne/tc
```

The 'modules' file is line oriented. In its simplest form each line contains the name of the module, whitespace, and the directory where the module resides. The directory is a path relative to $CVSROOT. The last four lines in the example above are examples of such lines.

The line that defines the module called 'modules' uses features that are not explained here. See Section C.1 [modules], page 159, for a full explanation of all the available features.

2.4.1 Editing administrative files

You edit the administrative files in the same way that you would edit any other module. Use 'cvs checkout CVSROOT' to get a working copy, edit it, and commit your changes in the normal way.

It is possible to commit an erroneous administrative file. You can often fix the error and check in a new revision, but sometimes a particularly bad error in the administrative file makes it impossible to commit new revisions.

2.5 Multiple repositories

In some situations it is a good idea to have more than one repository, for instance if you have two development groups that work on separate projects without sharing any code. All you have to do to have several repositories is to specify the appropriate repository, using the CVSROOT environment variable, the '-d' option to CVS, or (once you have checked out a working directory) by simply allowing CVS to use the repository that was used to check out the working directory (see Section 2.1 [Specifying a repository], page 11).

The big advantage of having multiple repositories is that they can reside on different servers. With CVS version 1.10, a single command cannot recurse into directories from different repositories. With development versions of CVS, you can check out code from multiple servers into your working directory. CVS will recurse and handle all the details of making connections to as many server machines as necessary to perform the requested command. Here is an example of how to set up a working directory:

```
cvs -d server1:/cvs co dir1
cd dir1
cvs -d server2:/root co sdir
cvs update
```

The cvs co commands set up the working directory, and then the cvs update command will contact server2, to update the dir1/sdir subdirectory, and server1, to update everything else.

2.6 Creating a repository

To set up a CVS repository, first choose the machine and disk on which you want to store the revision history of the source files. CPU and memory requirements are modest, so most machines should be adequate. For details see Section 2.9.1 [Server requirements], page 27.

To estimate disk space requirements, if you are importing RCS files from another system, the size of those files is the approximate initial size of your repository, or if you are starting without any version history, a rule of thumb is to allow for the server approximately three times the size of the code to be under CVS for the repository (you will eventually outgrow this, but not for a while). On the machines on which the developers will be working, you'll want disk space for approximately one working directory for each developer (either the entire tree or a portion of it, depending on what each developer uses).

The repository should be accessible (directly or via a networked file system) from all machines which want to use CVS in server or local mode; the client machines need not have any access to it other than via the CVS protocol. It is not possible to use CVS to read from a repository which one only has read access to; CVS needs to be able to create lock files (see Section 10.5 [Concurrency], page 84).

To create a repository, run the cvs init command. It will set up an empty repository in the CVS root specified in the usual way (see Chapter 2 [Repository], page 11). For example,

```
cvs -d /usr/local/cvsroot init
```

cvs init is careful to never overwrite any existing files in the repository, so no harm is done if you run cvs init on an already set-up repository.

cvs init will enable history logging; if you don't want that, remove the history file after running cvs init. See Section C.11 [history file], page 173.

2.7 Backing up a repository

There is nothing particularly magical about the files in the repository; for the most part it is possible to back them up just like any other files. However, there are a few issues to consider.

The first is that to be paranoid, one should either not use CVS during the backup, or have the backup program lock CVS while doing the backup. To not use CVS, you might forbid logins to machines which can access the repository, turn off your CVS server, or similar mechanisms. The details would depend on your operating system and how you have CVS set up. To lock CVS, you would create '#cvs.rfl' locks in each repository directory. See Section 10.5 [Concurrency], page 84, for more on CVS locks. Having said all this, if you just back up without any of these precautions, the results are unlikely to be particularly dire. Restoring from backup, the repository might be in an inconsistent state, but this would not be particularly hard to fix manually.

When you restore a repository from backup, assuming that changes in the repository were made after the time of the backup, working directories which were not affected by the failure may refer to revisions which no longer exist in the repository. Trying to run CVS in such directories will typically produce an error message. One way to get those changes back into the repository is as follows:

- Get a new working directory.
- Copy the files from the working directory from before the failure over to the new working directory (do not copy the contents of the 'CVS' directories, of course).
- Working in the new working directory, use commands such as cvs update and cvs diff to figure out what has changed, and then when you are ready, commit the changes into the repository.

2.8 Moving a repository

Just as backing up the files in the repository is pretty much like backing up any other files, if you need to move a repository from one place to another it is also pretty much like just moving any other collection of files.

The main thing to consider is that working directories point to the repository. The simplest way to deal with a moved repository is to just get a fresh working directory after the move. Of course, you'll want to make sure that the old working directory had been checked in before the move, or you figured out some other way to make sure that you don't lose any changes. If you really do want to reuse the existing working directory, it should be possible with manual surgery on the 'CVS/Repository' files. You can see Section 2.3 [Working directory storage], page 19, for information on the 'CVS/Repository' and 'CVS/Root' files, but unless you are sure you want to bother, it probably isn't worth it.

2.9 Remote repositories

Your working copy of the sources can be on a different machine than the repository. Using CVS in this manner is known as *client/server* operation. You run CVS on a machine which can mount your working directory, known as the *client*, and tell it to communicate to a machine which can mount the repository, known as the *server*. Generally, using a remote repository is just like using a local one, except that the format of the repository name is:

> :*method*:*user*@*hostname*:/path/to/repository

The details of exactly what needs to be set up depend on how you are connecting to the server.

If *method* is not specified, and the repository name contains ':', then the default is ext or server, depending on your platform; both are described in Section 2.9.2 [Connecting via rsh], page 28.

2.9.1 Server requirements

The quick answer to what sort of machine is suitable as a server is that requirements are modest—a server with 32M of memory or even less can handle a fairly large source tree with a fair amount of activity.

The real answer, of course, is more complicated. Estimating the known areas of large memory consumption should be sufficient to estimate memory requirements. There are two such areas documented here; other memory consumption should be small by comparison (if you find that is not the case, let us know, as described in Appendix H [BUGS], page 195, so we can update this documentation).

The first area of big memory consumption is large checkouts, when using the CVS server. The server consists of two processes for each client that it is serving. Memory consumption on the child process should remain fairly small. Memory consumption on the parent process, particularly if the network connection to the client is slow, can be expected to grow to slightly more than the size of the sources in a single directory, or two megabytes, whichever is larger.

Multiplying the size of each CVS server by the number of servers which you expect to have active at one time should give an idea of memory requirements for the server. For the most part, the memory consumed by the parent process probably can be swap space rather than physical memory.

The second area of large memory consumption is diff, when checking in large files. This is required even for binary files. The rule of thumb is to allow about ten times the size of the largest file you will want to check in, although five times may be adequate. For example, if you want to check in a file which is 10 megabytes, you should have 100 megabytes of memory on the machine doing the checkin (the server machine for client/server, or the machine running CVS for non-client/server). This can be swap space rather than physical memory. Because the memory is only required briefly, there is no particular need to allow memory for more than one such checkin at a time.

Resource consumption for the client is even more modest—any machine with enough capacity to run the operating system in question should have little trouble.

For information on disk space requirements, see Section 2.6 [Creating a repository], page 25.

2.9.2 Connecting with rsh

CVS uses the 'rsh' protocol[1] to perform these operations, so the remote user host needs to have a '.rhosts' file which grants access to the local user.

For example, suppose you are the user 'mozart' on the local machine 'toe.example.com', and the server machine is 'faun.example.org'. On faun, put the following line into the file '.rhosts' in 'bach''s home directory:

        toe.example.com mozart

Then test that rsh is working with

        rsh -l bach faun.example.org 'echo $PATH'

Next you have to make sure that rsh will be able to find the server. Make sure that the path which rsh printed in the above example includes the directory containing a program named cvs which is the server. You need to set the path in '.bashrc', '.cshrc', etc., not '.login' or '.profile'. Alternately, you can set the environment variable CVS_SERVER on the client machine to the filename of the server you want to use, for example '/usr/local/bin/cvs-1.6'.

There is no need to edit 'inetd.conf' or start a CVS server daemon.

There are two access methods that you use in CVSROOT for rsh. :server: specifies an internal rsh client, which is supported only by some CVS ports. :ext: specifies an external rsh program. By default this is rsh but you may set the CVS_RSH environment variable to invoke another program which can access the remote server (for example, remsh on HP-UX 9 because rsh is something different). It must be a program which can transmit data to and from the server without modifying it; for example the Windows NT rsh is not suitable since it by default translates between CRLF and LF. The OS/2 CVS port has a hack to pass '-b' to rsh to get around this, but since this could potentially cause problems for programs

---

[1] Publisher's note: in the time since this manual was written rsh has been superceded by the secure ssh protocol in most operating systems. When using CVS ssh is backwards-compatible with rsh as a drop-in replacement.

other than the standard rsh, it may change in the future. If you set CVS_
RSH to ssh or some other rsh replacement, the instructions in the rest of
this section concerning '.rhosts' and so on are likely to be inapplicable;
consult the documentation for your rsh replacement.

Continuing our example, supposing you want to access the module 'foo' in
the repository '/usr/local/cvsroot/', on machine 'faun.example.org',
you are ready to go:

```
cvs -d :ext:bach@faun.example.org:/usr/local/cvsroot
    checkout foo
```

(The 'bach@' can be omitted if the username is the same on both the local
and remote hosts.)

2.9.3 Direct connection with password authentication

The CVS client can also connect to the server using a password protocol.
This is particularly useful if using rsh is not feasible (for example, the
server is behind a firewall), and Kerberos also is not available.

To use this method, it is necessary to make some adjustments on both
the server and client sides.

2.9.3.1 Setting up the server for password authentication

First of all, you probably want to tighten the permissions on the
'$CVSROOT' and '$CVSROOT/CVSROOT' directories. See Section 2.9.3.3 [Pass-
word authentication security], page 33, for more details.

On the server side, the file '/etc/inetd.conf' needs to be edited so inetd
knows to run the command cvs pserver when it receives a connection on
the right port. By default, the port number is 2401; it would be different
if your client were compiled with CVS_AUTH_PORT defined to something
else, though.

If your inetd allows raw port numbers in '/etc/inetd.conf', then the
following (all on a single line in 'inetd.conf') should be sufficient:

```
2401  stream  tcp  nowait  root  /usr/local/bin/cvs
cvs -f --allow-root=/usr/cvsroot pserver
```

You could also use the '-T' option to specify a temporary directory.

The '--allow-root' option specifies the allowable CVSROOT directory.
Clients which attempt to use a different CVSROOT directory will not be
allowed to connect. If there is more than one CVSROOT directory which
you want to allow, repeat the option. (Unfortunately, many versions of
inetd have very small limits on the number of arguments and/or the

total length of the command. The usual solution to this problem is to have inetd run a shell script which then invokes CVS with the necessary arguments.)

If your inetd wants a symbolic service name instead of a raw port number, then put this in '/etc/services':

    cvspserver   2401/tcp

and put cvspserver instead of 2401 in 'inetd.conf'.

Once the above is taken care of, restart your inetd, or do whatever is necessary to force it to reread its initialization files.

If you are having trouble setting this up, see Section F.2 [Connection], page 190.

Because the client stores and transmits passwords in cleartext (almost— see Section 2.9.3.3 [Password authentication security], page 33, for details), a separate CVS password file is generally used, so people don't compromise their regular passwords when they access the repository. This file is '$CVSROOT/CVSROOT/passwd' (see Section 2.4 [Intro administrative files], page 23). It uses a colon-separated format, similar to '/etc/passwd' on Unix systems, except that it has fewer fields: CVS username, optional password, and an optional system username for CVS to run as if authentication succeeds. Here is an example 'passwd' file with five entries:

    anonymous:
    bach:ULtgRLXo7NRxs
    spwang:1s0p854gDF3DY
    melissa:tGX1fS8sun6rY:pubcvs
    qproj:XR4EZcEsOszik:pubcvs

(The passwords are encrypted according to the standard Unix crypt() function, so it is possible to paste in passwords directly from regular Unix '/etc/passwd' files.)

The first line in the example will grant access to any CVS client attempting to authenticate as user anonymous, no matter what password they use, including an empty password. (This is typical for sites granting anonymous read-only access; for information on how to do the "read-only" part, see See Section 2.10 [Read-only access], page 36.)

The second and third lines will grant access to bach and spwang if they supply their respective plaintext passwords.

The fourth line will grant access to melissa, if she supplies the correct password, but her CVS operations will actually run on the server side under the system user pubcvs. Thus, there need not be any system user named melissa, but there *must* be one named pubcvs.

The fifth line shows that system user identities can be shared: any client who successfully authenticates as qproj will actually run as pubcvs, just as melissa does. That way you could create a single, shared system user for each project in your repository, and give each developer their own line in the '$CVSROOT/CVSROOT/passwd' file. The CVS username on each line would be different, but the system username would be the same. The reason to have different CVS usernames is that CVS will log their actions under those names: when melissa commits a change to a project, the checkin is recorded in the project's history under the name melissa, not pubcvs. And the reason to have them share a system username is so that you can arrange permissions in the relevant area of the repository such that only that account has write-permission there.

If the system-user field is present, all password-authenticated CVS commands run as that user; if no system user is specified, CVS simply takes the CVS username as the system username and runs commands as that user. In either case, if there is no such user on the system, then the CVS operation will fail (regardless of whether the client supplied a valid password).

The password and system-user fields can both be omitted (and if the system-user field is omitted, then also omit the colon that would have separated it from the encrypted password). For example, this would be a valid '$CVSROOT/CVSROOT/passwd' file:

```
anonymous::pubcvs
fish:rKa5jzULzmhOo:kfogel
sussman:1sOp854gDF3DY
```

When the password field is omitted or empty, then the client's authentication attempt will succeed with any password, including the empty string. However, the colon after the CVS username is always necessary, even if the password is empty.

CVS can also fall back to use system authentication. When authenticating a password, the server first checks for the user in the '$CVSROOT/CVSROOT/passwd' file. If it finds the user, it will use that entry for authentication as described above. But if it does not find the user, or if the CVS 'passwd' file does not exist, then the server can try to authenticate the username and password using the operating system's user-lookup routines (this "fallback" behavior can be disabled by setting SystemAuth=no in the CVS 'config' file, see Section C.13 [config], page 174). Be aware, however, that falling back to system authentication might be a security risk: CVS operations would then be authenticated with that user's regular login password, and the password flies across the network in plaintext. See Section 2.9.3.3 [Password authentication security], page 33 for more on this.

Right now, the only way to put a password in the CVS 'passwd' file is to paste it there from somewhere else. Someday, there may be a cvs passwd command.

Unlike many of the files in '$CVSROOT/CVSROOT', it is normal to edit the 'passwd' file in-place, rather than via CVS. This is because of the possible security risks of having the 'passwd' file checked out to people's working copies. If you do want to include the 'passwd' file in checkouts of '$CVSROOT/CVSROOT', see See Section C.10 [checkoutlist], page 172.

2.9.3.2 Using the client with password authentication

To run a CVS command on a remote repository via the password-authenticating server, one specifies the pserver protocol, username, repository host, and path to the repository. For example:

```
cvs -d :pserver:bach@faun.example.org:/usr/local/cvsroot
    checkout someproj
```

or

```
CVSROOT=:pserver:bach@faun.example.org:/usr/local/cvsroot
cvs checkout someproj
```

However, unless you're connecting to a public-access repository (i.e., one where that username doesn't require a password), you'll need to *log in* first. Logging in verifies your password with the repository. It's done with the login command, which will prompt you interactively for the password:

```
cvs -d :pserver:bach@faun.example.org:/usr/local/cvsroot
    login
CVS password:
```

After you enter the password, CVS verifies it with the server. If the verification succeeds, then that combination of username, host, repository, and password is permanently recorded, so future transactions with that repository won't require you to run cvs login. (If verification fails, CVS will exit complaining that the password was incorrect, and nothing will be recorded.)

The records are stored, by default, in the file '$HOME/.cvspass'. That file's format is human-readable, and to a degree human-editable, but note that the passwords are not stored in cleartext—they are trivially encoded to protect them from "innocent" compromise (i.e., inadvertent viewing by a system administrator or other non-malicious person).

You can change the default location of this file by setting the CVS_PASSFILE environment variable. If you use this variable, make sure you set it *before* cvs login is run. If you were to set it after running cvs login, then later CVS commands would be unable to look up the password for transmission to the server.

Once you have logged in, all CVS commands using that remote repository and username will authenticate with the stored password. So, for example

```
cvs -d :pserver:bach@faun.example.org:/usr/local/cvsroot
   checkout foo
```

should just work (unless the password changes on the server side, in which case you'll have to re-run cvs login).

Note that if the ':pserver:' were not present in the repository specification, CVS would assume it should use rsh to connect with the server instead (see Section 2.9.2 [Connecting via rsh], page 28).

Of course, once you have a working copy checked out and are running CVS commands from within it, there is no longer any need to specify the repository explicitly, because CVS can deduce the repository from the working copy's 'CVS' subdirectory.

The password for a given remote repository can be removed from the CVS_PASSFILE by using the cvs logout command.

2.9.3.3 Security considerations with password authentication

The passwords are stored on the client side in a trivial encoding of the cleartext, and transmitted in the same encoding. The encoding is done only to prevent inadvertent password compromises (i.e., a system administrator accidentally looking at the file), and will not prevent even a naive attacker from gaining the password.

The separate CVS password file (see Section 2.9.3.1 [Password authentication server], page 29) allows people to use a different password for repository access than for login access. On the other hand, once a user has non-read-only access to the repository, she can execute programs on the server system through a variety of means. Thus, repository access implies fairly broad system access as well. It might be possible to modify CVS to prevent that, but no one has done so as of this writing.

Note that because the '$CVSROOT/CVSROOT' directory contains 'passwd' and other files which are used to check security, you must control the permissions on this directory as tightly as the permissions on '/etc'. The same applies to the '$CVSROOT' directory itself and any directory above it in the tree. Anyone who has write access to such a directory will have the ability to become any user on the system. Note that these permissions are typically tighter than you would use if you are not using pserver.

In summary, anyone who gets the password gets repository access (which may imply some measure of general system access as well). The password is available to anyone who can sniff network packets or read a protected (i.e., user read-only) file. If you want real security, get Kerberos.

2.9.4 Direct connection with GSSAPI

GSSAPI is a generic interface to network security systems such as Kerberos 5. If you have a working GSSAPI library, you can have CVS connect via a direct TCP connection, authenticating with GSSAPI.

To do this, CVS needs to be compiled with GSSAPI support; when configuring CVS it tries to detect whether GSSAPI libraries using kerberos version 5 are present. You can also use the '--with-gssapi' flag to configure.

The connection is authenticated using GSSAPI, but the message stream is *not* authenticated by default. You must use the -a global option to request stream authentication.

The data transmitted is *not* encrypted by default. Encryption support must be compiled into both the client and the server; use the '--enable-encrypt' configure option to turn it on. You must then use the -x global option to request encryption.

GSSAPI connections are handled on the server side by the same server which handles the password authentication server; see Section 2.9.3.1 [Password authentication server], page 29. If you are using a GSSAPI mechanism such as Kerberos which provides for strong authentication, you will probably want to disable the ability to authenticate via cleartext passwords. To do so, create an empty 'CVSROOT/passwd' password file, and set SystemAuth=no in the config file (see Section C.13 [config], page 174).

The GSSAPI server uses a principal name of cvs/*hostname*, where *hostname* is the canonical name of the server host. You will have to set this up as required by your GSSAPI mechanism.

To connect using GSSAPI, use ':gserver:'. For example,

```
cvs -d :gserver:faun.example.org:/usr/local/cvsroot
  checkout foo
```

2.9.5 Direct connection with kerberos

The easiest way to use kerberos is to use the kerberos rsh, as described in Section 2.9.2 [Connecting via rsh], page 28. The main disadvantage of using rsh is that all the data needs to pass through additional programs, so it may be slower. So if you have kerberos installed you can connect via a direct TCP connection, authenticating with kerberos.

This section concerns the kerberos network security system, version 4. Kerberos version 5 is supported via the GSSAPI generic network security interface, as described in the previous section.

To do this, CVS needs to be compiled with kerberos support; when configuring CVS it tries to detect whether kerberos is present or you can use the '--with-krb4' flag to configure.

The data transmitted is *not* encrypted by default. Encryption support must be compiled into both the client and server; use the '--enable-encryption' configure option to turn it on. You must then use the -x global option to request encryption.

You need to edit 'inetd.conf' on the server machine to run cvs kserver. The client uses port 1999 by default; if you want to use another port specify it in the CVS_CLIENT_PORT environment variable on the client.

When you want to use CVS, get a ticket in the usual way (generally kinit); it must be a ticket which allows you to log into the server machine. Then you are ready to go:

```
cvs -d :kserver:faun.example.org:/usr/local/cvsroot
    checkout foo
```

Previous versions of CVS would fall back to a connection via rsh; this version will not do so.

2.9.6 Connecting with fork

This access method allows you to connect to a repository on your local disk via the remote protocol. In other words it does pretty much the same thing as :local:, but various quirks, bugs and the like are those of the remote CVS rather than the local CVS.

For day-to-day operations you might prefer either :local: or :fork:, depending on your preferences. Of course :fork: comes in particularly handy in testing or debugging cvs and the remote protocol. Specifically, we avoid all of the network-related setup/configuration, timeouts, and authentication inherent in the other remote access methods but still create a connection which uses the remote protocol.

To connect using the fork method, use ':fork:' and the pathname to your local repository. For example:

```
cvs -d :fork:/usr/local/cvsroot checkout foo
```

As with :ext:, the server is called 'cvs' by default, or the value of the CVS_SERVER environment variable.

2.10 Read-only repository access

It is possible to grant read-only repository access to people using the password-authenticated server (see Section 2.9.3 [Password authenticated], page 29). (The other access methods do not have explicit support for read-only users because those methods all assume login access to the repository machine anyway, and therefore the user can do whatever local file permissions allow her to do.)

A user who has read-only access can do only those CVS operations which do not modify the repository, except for certain "administrative" files (such as lock files and the history file). It may be desirable to use this feature in conjunction with user-aliasing (see Section 2.9.3.1 [Password authentication server], page 29).

Unlike with previous versions of CVS, read-only users should be able merely to read the repository, and not to execute programs on the server or otherwise gain unexpected levels of access. Or to be more accurate, the *known* holes have been plugged. Because this feature is new and has not received a comprehensive security audit, you should use whatever level of caution seems warranted given your attitude concerning security.

There are two ways to specify read-only access for a user: by inclusion, and by exclusion.

"Inclusion" means listing that user specifically in the '$CVSROOT/CVSROOT/readers' file, which is simply a newline-separated list of users. Here is a sample 'readers' file:

```
melissa
splotnik
jrandom
```

(Don't forget the newline after the last user.)

"Exclusion" means explicitly listing everyone who has *write* access—if the file

```
$CVSROOT/CVSROOT/writers
```

exists, then only those users listed in it have write access, and everyone else has read-only access (of course, even the read-only users still need to be listed in the CVS 'passwd' file). The 'writers' file has the same format as the 'readers' file.

Note: if your CVS 'passwd' file maps cvs users onto system users (see Section 2.9.3.1 [Password authentication server], page 29), make sure you deny or grant read-only access using the *cvs* usernames, not the system usernames. That is, the 'readers' and 'writers' files contain cvs usernames, which may or may not be the same as system usernames.

Here is a complete description of the server's behavior in deciding whether to grant read-only or read-write access:

If 'readers' exists, and this user is listed in it, then she gets read-only access. Or if 'writers' exists, and this user is NOT listed in it, then she also gets read-only access (this is true even if 'readers' exists but she is not listed there). Otherwise, she gets full read-write access.

Of course there is a conflict if the user is listed in both files. This is resolved in the more conservative way, it being better to protect the repository too much than too little: such a user gets read-only access.

2.11 Temporary directories for the server

While running, the CVS server creates temporary directories. They are named

> cvs-serv*pid*

where *pid* is the process identification number of the server. They are located in the directory specified by the TMPDIR environment variable (see Appendix D [Environment variables], page 177), the '-T' global option (see Section A.4 [Global options], page 109), or failing that '/tmp'.

In most cases the server will remove the temporary directory when it is done, whether it finishes normally or abnormally. However, there are a few cases in which the server does not or cannot remove the temporary directory, for example:

- If the server aborts due to an internal server error, it may preserve the directory to aid in debugging

- If the server is killed in a way that it has no way of cleaning up (most notably, 'kill -KILL' on unix).

- If the system shuts down without an orderly shutdown, which tells the server to clean up.

In cases such as this, you will need to manually remove the 'cvs-serv*pid*' directories. As long as there is no server running with process identification number *pid*, it is safe to do so.

3 Starting a project with CVS

Because renaming files and moving them between directories is somewhat inconvenient, the first thing you do when you start a new project should be to think through your file organization. It is not impossible to rename or move files, but it does increase the potential for confusion and CVS does have some quirks particularly in the area of renaming directories. See Section 7.4 [Moving files], page 68.

What to do next depends on the situation at hand.

3.1 Setting up the files

The first step is to create the files inside the repository. This can be done in a couple of different ways.

3.1.1 Creating a directory tree from a number of files

When you begin using CVS, you will probably already have several projects that can be put under CVS control. In these cases the easiest way is to use the `import` command. An example is probably the easiest way to explain how to use it. If the files you want to install in CVS reside in '*wdir*', and you want them to appear in the repository as '`$CVSROOT/yoyodyne/`*rdir*', you can do this:

```
$ cd wdir
$ cvs import -m "Imported sources" yoyodyne/rdir
      yoyo start
```

Unless you supply a log message with the '-m' flag, CVS starts an editor and prompts for a message. The string 'yoyo' is a *vendor tag*, and '`start`' is a *release tag*. They may fill no purpose in this context, but since CVS requires them they must be present. See Chapter 13 [Tracking sources], page 99, for more information about them.

You can now verify that it worked, and remove your original source directory.

```
$ cd ..
$ cvs checkout yoyodyne/rdir        # Explanation below
$ diff -r wdir yoyodyne/rdir
$ rm -r wdir
```

Erasing the original sources is a good idea, to make sure that you do not accidentally edit them in *wdir*, bypassing CVS. Of course, it would be wise to make sure that you have a backup of the sources before you remove them.

The checkout command can either take a module name as argument (as it has done in all previous examples) or a path name relative to $CVSROOT, as it did in the example above.

It is a good idea to check that the permissions CVS sets on the directories inside $CVSROOT are reasonable, and that they belong to the proper groups. See Section 2.2.2 [File permissions], page 14.

If some of the files you want to import are binary, you may want to use the wrappers features to specify which files are binary and which are not. See Section C.2 [Wrappers], page 163.

3.1.2 Creating Files From Other Version Control Systems

If you have a project which you are maintaining with another version control system, such as RCS, you may wish to put the files from that project into CVS, and preserve the revision history of the files.

From RCS If you have been using RCS, find the RCS files—usually a file named 'foo.c' will have its RCS file in 'RCS/foo.c,v' (but it could be other places; consult the RCS documentation for details). Then create the appropriate directories in CVS if they do not already exist. Then copy the files into the appropriate directories in the CVS repository (the name in the repository must be the name of the source file with ',v' added; the files go directly in the appropriate directory of the repository, not in an 'RCS' subdirectory). This is one of the few times when it is a good idea to access the CVS repository directly, rather than using CVS commands. Then you are ready to check out a new working directory.

The RCS file should not be locked when you move it into CVS; if it is, CVS will have trouble letting you operate on it.

From another version control system

Many version control systems have the ability to export RCS files in the standard format. If yours does, export the RCS files and then follow the above instructions.

Failing that, probably your best bet is to write a script that will check out the files one revision at a time using the command line interface to the other system, and then check the revisions into CVS. The 'sccs2rcs' script mentioned below may be a useful example to follow.

From SCCS

> There is a script in the 'contrib' directory of the CVS source distribution called 'sccs2rcs' which converts SCCS files to RCS files. Note: you must run it on a machine which has both SCCS and RCS installed, and like everything else in contrib it is unsupported (your mileage may vary).

From PVCS

> There is a script in the 'contrib' directory of the CVS source distribution called 'pvcs_to_rcs' which converts PVCS archives to RCS files. You must run it on a machine which has both PVCS and RCS installed, and like everything else in contrib it is unsupported (your mileage may vary). See the comments in the script for details.

3.1.3 Creating a directory tree from scratch

For a new project, the easiest thing to do is probably to create an empty directory structure, like this:

```
$ mkdir tc
$ mkdir tc/man
$ mkdir tc/testing
```

After that, you use the import command to create the corresponding (empty) directory structure inside the repository:

```
$ cd tc
$ cvs import -m "Created directory structure"
    yoyodyne/dir yoyo start
```

Then, use add to add files (and new directories) as they appear.

Check that the permissions CVS sets on the directories inside $CVSROOT are reasonable.

3.2 Defining the module

The next step is to define the module in the 'modules' file. This is not strictly necessary, but modules can be convenient in grouping together related files and directories.

In simple cases these steps are sufficient to define a module.

1. Get a working copy of the modules file.

   ```
   $ cvs checkout CVSROOT/modules
   $ cd CVSROOT
   ```

2. Edit the file and insert a line that defines the module. See Section 2.4 [Intro administrative files], page 23, for an introduction. See

Section C.1 [modules], page 159, for a full description of the modules file. You can use the following line to define the module 'tc':

```
tc    yoyodyne/tc  ·
```

3. Commit your changes to the modules file.

```
$ cvs commit -m "Added the tc module." modules
```

4. Release the modules module.

```
$ cd ..
$ cvs release -d CVSROOT
```

4 Revisions

For many uses of CVS, one doesn't need to worry too much about revision numbers; CVS assigns numbers such as 1.1, 1.2, and so on, and that is all one needs to know. However, some people prefer to have more knowledge and control concerning how CVS assigns revision numbers.

If one wants to keep track of a set of revisions involving more than one file, such as which revisions went into a particular release, one uses a *tag*, which is a symbolic revision which can be assigned to a numeric revision in each file.

4.1 Revision numbers

Each version of a file has a unique *revision number*. Revision numbers look like '1.1', '1.2', '1.3.2.2' or even '1.3.2.2.4.5'. A revision number always has an even number of period-separated decimal integers. By default revision 1.1 is the first revision of a file. Each successive revision is given a new number by increasing the rightmost number by one. The following figure displays a few revisions, with newer revisions to the right.

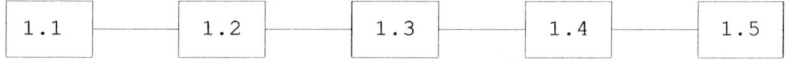

It is also possible to end up with numbers containing more than one period, for example '1.3.2.2'. Such revisions represent revisions on branches (see Chapter 5 [Branching and merging], page 53); such revision numbers are explained in detail in Section 5.4 [Branches and revisions], page 55.

4.2 Versions, revisions and releases

A file can have several versions, as described above. Likewise, a software product can have several versions. A software product is often given a version number such as '4.1.1'.

Versions in the first sense are called *revisions* in this document, and versions in the second sense are called *releases*. To avoid confusion, the word *version* is almost never used in this document.

4.3 Assigning revisions

By default, CVS will assign numeric revisions by leaving the first number the same and incrementing the second number. For example, 1.1, 1.2, 1.3, etc.

When adding a new file, the second number will always be one and the first number will equal the highest first number of any file in that directory. For example, the current directory contains files whose highest numbered revisions are 1.7, 3.1, and 4.12, then an added file will be given the numeric revision 4.1.

Normally there is no reason to care about the revision numbers—it is easier to treat them as internal numbers that CVS maintains, and tags provide a better way to distinguish between things like release 1 versus release 2 of your product (see Section 4.4 [Tags], page 44). However, if you want to set the numeric revisions, the '-r' option to cvs commit can do that. The '-r' option implies the '-f' option, in the sense that it causes the files to be committed even if they are not modified.

For example, to bring all your files up to revision 3.0 (including those that haven't changed), you might invoke:

```
$ cvs commit -r 3.0
```

Note that the number you specify with '-r' must be larger than any existing revision number. That is, if revision 3.0 exists, you cannot 'cvs commit -r 1.3'. If you want to maintain several releases in parallel, you need to use a branch (see Chapter 5 [Branching and merging], page 53).

4.4 Tags–Symbolic revisions

The revision numbers live a life of their own. They need not have anything at all to do with the release numbers of your software product. Depending on how you use CVS the revision numbers might change several times between two releases. As an example, some of the source files that make up RCS 5.6 have the following revision numbers:

ci.c	5.21
co.c	5.9
ident.c	5.3
rcs.c	5.12
rcsbase.h	5.11
rcsdiff.c	5.10
rcsedit.c	5.11
rcsfcmp.c	5.9
rcsgen.c	5.10
rcslex.c	5.11
rcsmap.c	5.2
rcsutil.c	5.10

You can use the tag command to give a symbolic name to a certain revision of a file. You can use the '-v' flag to the status command to see all tags that a file has, and which revision numbers they represent. Tag names must start with an uppercase or lowercase letter and can contain uppercase and lowercase letters, digits, '-', and '_'. The two tag names BASE and HEAD are reserved for use by CVS. It is expected that future names which are special to CVS will be specially named, for example by starting with '.', rather than being named analogously to BASE and HEAD, to avoid conflicts with actual tag names.

You'll want to choose some convention for naming tags, based on information such as the name of the program and the version number of the release. For example, one might take the name of the program, immediately followed by the version number with '.' changed to '-', so that CVS 1.9 would be tagged with the name cvs1-9. If you choose a consistent convention, then you won't constantly be guessing whether a tag is cvs-1-9 or cvs1_9 or what. You might even want to consider enforcing your convention in the taginfo file (see Section 8.3 [user-defined logging], page 73).

The following example shows how you can add a tag to a file. The commands must be issued inside your working directory. That is, you should issue the command in the directory where 'backend.c' resides.

```
$ cvs tag rel-0-4 backend.c
T backend.c
$ cvs status -v backend.c
=======================================================
File: backend.c          Status: Up-to-date

Version:        1.4  Tue Dec  1 14:39:01 1992
RCS Version:    1.4  /u/cvsroot/yoyodyne/tc/backend.c,v
Sticky Tag:     (none)
Sticky Date:    (none)
Sticky Options: (none)

Existing Tags:
rel-0-4         (revision: 1.4)
```

For a complete summary of the syntax of cvs tag, including the various options, see Appendix B [Invoking CVS], page 145.

There is seldom reason to tag a file in isolation. A more common use is to tag all the files that constitute a module with the same tag at strategic points in the development life-cycle, such as when a release is made.

```
$ cvs tag rel-1-0 .
cvs tag: Tagging .
T Makefile
```

```
T backend.c
T driver.c
T frontend.c
T parser.c
```

(When you give CVS a directory as argument, it generally applies the operation to all the files in that directory, and (recursively), to any subdirectories that it may contain. See Chapter 6 [Recursive behavior], page 63.)

The **checkout** command has a flag, '-r', that lets you check out a certain revision of a module. This flag makes it easy to retrieve the sources that make up release 1.0 of the module 'tc' at any time in the future:

```
$ cvs checkout -r rel-1-0 tc
```

This is useful, for instance, if someone claims that there is a bug in that release, but you cannot find the bug in the current working copy.

You can also check out a module as it was at any given date. See Section A.7.1 [checkout options], page 121. When specifying '-r' to any of these commands, you will need beware of sticky tags; see Section 4.9 [Sticky tags], page 50.

When you tag more than one file with the same tag you can think about the tag as "a curve drawn through a matrix of filename vs. revision number." Say we have 5 files with the following revisions:

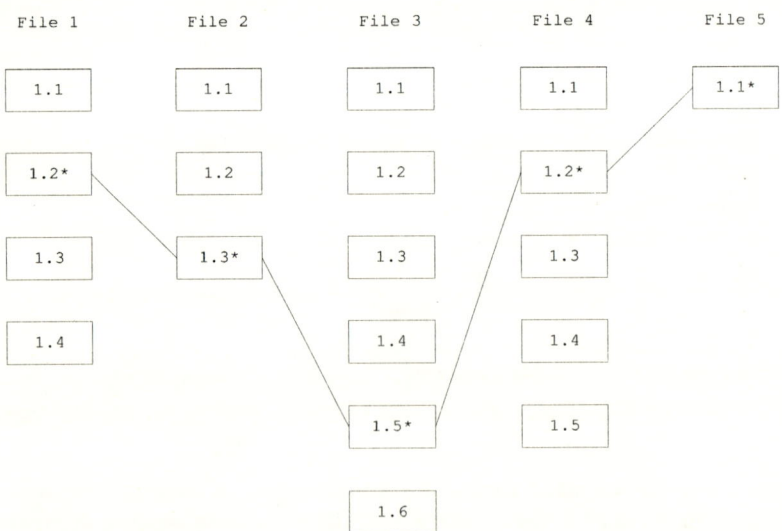

At some time in the past, the * versions were tagged. You can think of the tag as a handle attached to the curve drawn through the tagged revisions. When you pull on the handle, you get all the tagged revisions.

Another way to look at it is that you "sight" through a set of revisions that is "flat" along the tagged revisions, like this:

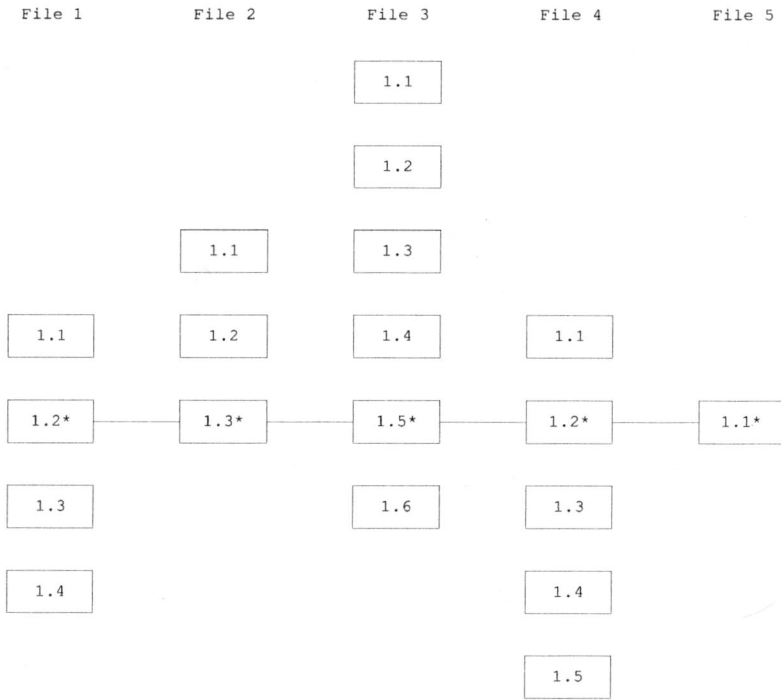

4.5 Specifying what to tag from the working directory

The example in the previous section demonstrates one of the most common ways to choose which revisions to tag. Namely, running the cvs tag command without arguments causes CVS to select the revisions which are checked out in the current working directory. For example, if the copy of 'backend.c' in working directory was checked out from revision 1.4, then CVS will tag revision 1.4. Note that the tag is applied immediately to revision 1.4 in the repository; tagging is not like modifying a file, or other operations in which one first modifies the working directory and then runs cvs commit to transfer that modification to the repository.

One potentially surprising aspect of the fact that cvs tag operates on the repository is that you are tagging the checked-in revisions, which may differ from locally modified files in your working directory. If you want to avoid doing this by mistake, specify the '-c' option to cvs tag. If there

are any locally modified files, CVS will abort with an error before it tags
any files:

```
$ cvs tag -c rel-0-4
cvs tag: backend.c is locally modified
cvs [tag aborted]: correct the above errors first!
```

4.6 Specifying what to tag by date or revision

The **cvs rtag** command tags the repository as of a certain date or time
(or can be used to tag the latest revision). **rtag** works directly on the
repository contents (it requires no prior checkout and does not look for a
working directory).

The following options specify which date or revision to tag. See Section A.5 [Common options], page 111, for a complete description of them.

-D *date*   Tag the most recent revision no later than *date*.

-f   Only useful with the '-D *date*' or '-r *tag*' flags. If no match-
               ing revision is found, use the most recent revision (instead
               of ignoring the file).

-r *tag*   Only tag those files that contain existing tag *tag*.

The **cvs tag** command also allows one to specify files by revision or date,
using the same '-r', '-D', and '-f' options. However, this feature is probably not what you want. The reason is that **cvs tag** chooses which files to
tag based on the files that exist in the working directory, rather than the
files which existed as of the given tag/date. Therefore, you are generally
better off using **cvs rtag**. The exceptions might be cases like:

```
cvs tag -r 1.4 backend.c
```

4.7 Deleting, moving, and renaming tags

Normally one does not modify tags. They exist in order to record the
history of the repository and so deleting them or changing their meaning
would, generally, not be what you want.

However, there might be cases in which one uses a tag temporarily or accidentally puts one in the wrong place. Therefore, one might delete, move,
or rename a tag. Warning: the commands in this section are dangerous; they permanently discard historical information and it can difficult
or impossible to recover from errors. If you are a CVS administrator, you
may consider restricting these commands with taginfo (see Section 8.3
[user-defined logging], page 73).

To delete a tag, specify the '-d' option to either cvs tag or cvs rtag. For example:

```
cvs rtag -d rel-0-4 tc
```

deletes the tag rel-0-4 from the module tc.

When we say *move* a tag, we mean to make the same name point to different revisions. For example, the stable tag may currently point to revision 1.4 of 'backend.c' and perhaps we want to make it point to revision 1.6. To move a tag, specify the '-F' option to either cvs tag or cvs rtag. For example, the task just mentioned might be accomplished as:

```
cvs tag -r 1.6 -F stable backend.c
```

When we say *rename* a tag, we mean to make a different name point to the same revisions as the old tag. For example, one may have misspelled the tag name and want to correct it (hopefully before others are relying on the old spelling). To rename a tag, first create a new tag using the '-r' option to cvs rtag, and then delete the old name. This leaves the new tag on exactly the same files as the old tag. For example:

```
cvs rtag -r old-name-0-4 rel-0-4 tc
cvs rtag -d old-name-0-4 tc
```

4.8 Tagging and adding and removing files

The subject of exactly how tagging interacts with adding and removing files is somewhat obscure; for the most part CVS will keep track of whether files exist or not without too much fussing. By default, tags are applied to only files which have a revision corresponding to what is being tagged. Files which did not exist yet, or which were already removed, simply omit the tag, and CVS knows to treat the absence of a tag as meaning that the file didn't exist as of that tag.

However, this can lose a small amount of information. For example, suppose a file was added and then removed. Then, if the tag is missing for that file, there is no way to know whether the tag refers to the time before the file was added, or the time after it was removed. If you specify the '-r' option to cvs rtag, then CVS tags the files which have been removed, and thereby avoids this problem. For example, one might specify -r HEAD to tag the head.

On the subject of adding and removing files, the cvs rtag command has a '-a' option which means to clear the tag from removed files that would not otherwise be tagged. For example, one might specify this option in conjunction with '-F' when moving a tag. If one moved a tag without '-a', then the tag in the removed files might still refer to the old revision,

rather than reflecting the fact that the file had been removed. I don't
think this is necessary if '-r' is specified, as noted above.

4.9 Sticky tags

Sometimes a working copy's revision has extra data associated with it, for
example it might be on a branch (see Chapter 5 [Branching and merging],
page 53), or restricted to versions prior to a certain date by 'checkout
-D' or 'update -D'. Because this data persists – that is, it applies to
subsequent commands in the working copy – we refer to it as *sticky*.

Most of the time, stickiness is an obscure aspect of CVS that you don't
need to think about. However, even if you don't want to use the feature,
you may need to know *something* about sticky tags (for example, how to
avoid them!).

You can use the **status** command to see if any sticky tags or dates are
set:

```
$ cvs status driver.c
===================================================
File: driver.c          Status: Up-to-date

Version:        1.7.2.1 Sat Dec  5 19:35:03 1992
RCS Version:    1.7.2.1 /u/cvsroot/yoyodyne/tc/driver.c,v
Sticky Tag:     rel-1-0-patches (branch: 1.7.2)
Sticky Date:    (none)
Sticky Options: (none)
```

The sticky tags will remain on your working files until you delete them
with 'cvs update -A'. The '-A' option retrieves the version of the file
from the head of the trunk, and forgets any sticky tags, dates, or options.

The most common use of sticky tags is to identify which branch one is
working on, as described in Section 5.3 [Accessing branches], page 54.
However, non-branch sticky tags have uses as well. For example, suppose
that you want to avoid updating your working directory, to isolate yourself
from possibly destabilizing changes other people are making. You can, of
course, just refrain from running **cvs update**. But if you want to avoid
updating only a portion of a larger tree, then sticky tags can help. If you
check out a certain revision (such as 1.4) it will become sticky. Subsequent
cvs update commands will not retrieve the latest revision until you reset
the tag with **cvs update -A**. Likewise, use of the '-D' option to **update**
or **checkout** sets a *sticky date*, which, similarly, causes that date to be
used for future retrievals.

People often want to retrieve an old version of a file without setting a
sticky tag. This can be done with the '-p' option to checkout or update,
which sends the contents of the file to standard output. For example:

```
$ cvs update -p -r 1.1 file1 >file1
===========================================================
Checking out file1
RCS:  /tmp/cvs-sanity/cvsroot/first-dir/Attic/file1,v
VERS: 1.1
***************
$
```

However, this isn't the easiest way, if you are asking how to undo a previous checkin (in this example, put 'file1' back to the way it was as
of revision 1.1). In that case you are better off using the '-j' option
to update; for further discussion see Section 5.8 [Merging two revisions],
page 59.

5 Branching and merging

CVS allows you to isolate changes onto a separate line of development, known as a *branch*. When you change files on a branch, those changes do not appear on the main trunk or other branches.

Later you can move changes from one branch to another branch (or the main trunk) by *merging*. Merging involves first running **cvs update -j**, to merge the changes into the working directory. You can then commit that revision, and thus effectively copy the changes onto another branch.

5.1 What branches are good for

Suppose that release 1.0 of tc has been made. You are continuing to develop tc, planning to create release 1.1 in a couple of months. After a while your customers start to complain about a fatal bug. You check out release 1.0 (see Section 4.4 [Tags], page 44) and find the bug (which turns out to have a trivial fix). However, the current revision of the sources are in a state of flux and are not expected to be stable for at least another month. There is no way to make a bugfix release based on the newest sources.

The thing to do in a situation like this is to create a *branch* on the revision trees for all the files that make up release 1.0 of tc. You can then make modifications to the branch without disturbing the main trunk. When the modifications are finished you can elect to either incorporate them on the main trunk, or leave them on the branch.

5.2 Creating a branch

You can create a branch with **tag -b**; for example, assuming you're in a working copy:

```
$ cvs tag -b rel-1-0-patches
```

This splits off a branch based on the current revisions in the working copy, assigning that branch the name 'rel-1-0-patches'.

It is important to understand that branches get created in the repository, not in the working copy. Creating a branch based on current revisions, as the above example does, will *not* automatically switch the working copy to be on the new branch. For information on how to do that, see Section 5.3 [Accessing branches], page 54.

You can also create a branch without reference to any working copy, by using **rtag**:

```
$ cvs rtag -b -r rel-1-0 rel-1-0-patches tc
```

'-r rel-1-0' says that this branch should be rooted at the revision that corresponds to the tag 'rel-1-0'. It need not be the most recent revision – it's often useful to split a branch off an old revision (for example, when fixing a bug in a past release otherwise known to be stable).

As with 'tag', the '-b' flag tells rtag to create a branch (rather than just a symbolic revision name). Note that the numeric revision number that matches 'rel-1-0' will probably be different from file to file.

So, the full effect of the command is to create a new branch – named 'rel-1-0-patches' – in module 'tc', rooted in the revision tree at the point tagged by 'rel-1-0'.

5.3 Accessing branches

You can retrieve a branch in one of two ways: by checking it out fresh from the repository, or by switching an existing working copy over to the branch.

To check out a branch from the repository, invoke 'checkout' with the '-r' flag, followed by the tag name of the branch (see Section 5.2 [Creating a branch], page 53):

```
$ cvs checkout -r rel-1-0-patches tc
```

Or, if you already have a working copy, you can switch it to a given branch with 'update -r':

```
$ cvs update -r rel-1-0-patches tc
```

or equivalently:

```
$ cd tc
$ cvs update -r rel-1-0-patches
```

It does not matter if the working copy was originally on the main trunk or on some other branch – the above command will switch it to the named branch. And similarly to a regular 'update' command, 'update -r' merges any changes you have made, notifying you of conflicts where they occur.

Once you have a working copy tied to a particular branch, it remains there until you tell it otherwise. This means that changes checked in from the working copy will add new revisions on that branch, while leaving the main trunk and other branches unaffected.

To find out what branch a working copy is on, you can use the 'status' command. In its output, look for the field named 'Sticky tag' (see Section 4.9 [Sticky tags], page 50) – that's CVS's way of telling you the branch, if any, of the current working files:

```
$ cvs status -v driver.c backend.c
===================================================
File: driver.c          Status: Up-to-date
```

```
Version:          1.7  Sat Dec  5 18:25:54 1992
RCS Version:      1.7  /u/cvsroot/yoyodyne/tc/driver.c,v
Sticky Tag:       rel-1-0-patches (branch: 1.7.2)
Sticky Date:      (none)
Sticky Options:   (none)

Existing Tags:
  rel-1-0-patches            (branch: 1.7.2)
  rel-1-0                    (revision: 1.7)


========================================================
File: backend.c         Status: Up-to-date

Version:          1.4  Tue Dec  1 14:39:01 1992
RCS Version:      1.4  /u/cvsroot/yoyodyne/tc/backend.c,v
Sticky Tag:       rel-1-0-patches (branch: 1.4.2)
Sticky Date:      (none)
Sticky Options:   (none)

Existing Tags:
  rel-1-0-patches            (branch: 1.4.2)
  rel-1-0                    (revision: 1.4)
  rel-0-4                    (revision: 1.4)
```

Don't be confused by the fact that the branch numbers for each file are different ('1.7.2' and '1.4.2' respectively). The branch tag is the same, 'rel-1-0-patches', and the files are indeed on the same branch. The numbers simply reflect the point in each file's revision history at which the branch was made. In the above example, one can deduce that 'driver.c' had been through more changes than 'backend.c' before this branch was created.

See Section 5.4 [Branches and revisions], page 55 for details about how branch numbers are constructed.

5.4 Branches and revisions

Ordinarily, a file's revision history is a linear series of increments (see Section 4.1 [Revision numbers], page 43):

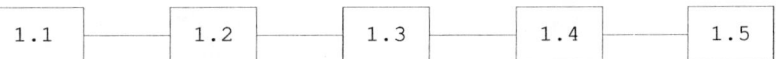

However, CVS is not limited to linear development. The *revision tree* can be split into *branches*, where each branch is a self-maintained line of development. Changes made on one branch can easily be moved back to the main trunk.

Each branch has a *branch number*, consisting of an odd number of period-separated decimal integers. The branch number is created by appending an integer to the revision number where the corresponding branch forked off. Having branch numbers allows more than one branch to be forked off from a certain revision.

All revisions on a branch have revision numbers formed by appending an ordinal number to the branch number. The following figure illustrates branching with an example.

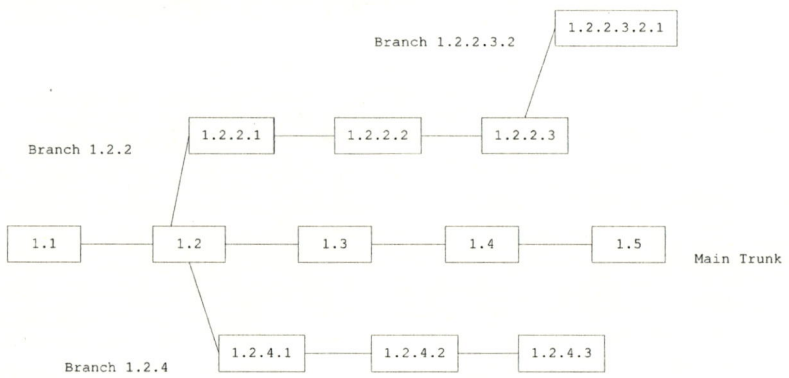

The exact details of how the branch number is constructed is not something you normally need to be concerned about, but here is how it works: When CVS creates a branch number it picks the first unused even integer, starting with 2. So when you want to create a branch from revision 6.4 it will be numbered 6.4.2. All branch numbers ending in a zero (such as 6.4.0) are used internally by CVS (see Section 5.5 [Magic branch numbers], page 56). The branch 1.1.1 has a special meaning. See Chapter 13 [Tracking sources], page 99.

5.5 Magic branch numbers

This section describes a CVS feature called *magic branches*. For most purposes, you need not worry about magic branches; CVS handles them for you. However, they are visible to you in certain circumstances, so it may be useful to have some idea of how it works.

Externally, branch numbers consist of an odd number of dot-separated decimal integers. See Section 4.1 [Revision numbers], page 43. That is not the whole truth, however. For efficiency reasons CVS sometimes inserts an extra 0 in the second rightmost position (1.2.4 becomes 1.2.0.4, 8.9.10.11.12 becomes 8.9.10.11.0.12 and so on).

CVS does a pretty good job at hiding these so called magic branches, but in a few places the hiding is incomplete:

- The magic branch number appears in the output from cvs log.
- You cannot specify a symbolic branch name to cvs admin.

You can use the admin command to reassign a symbolic name to a branch the way RCS expects it to be. If R4patches is assigned to the branch 1.4.2 (magic branch number 1.4.0.2) in file 'numbers.c' you can do this:

```
$ cvs admin -NR4patches:1.4.2 numbers.c
```

It only works if at least one revision is already committed on the branch. Be very careful so that you do not assign the tag to the wrong number. (There is no way to see how the tag was assigned yesterday).

5.6 Merging an entire branch

You can merge changes made on a branch into your working copy by giving the '-j branch' flag to the update command. With one '-j branch' option it merges the changes made between the point where the branch forked and newest revision on that branch (into your working copy).

The '-j' stands for "join".

Consider this revision tree:

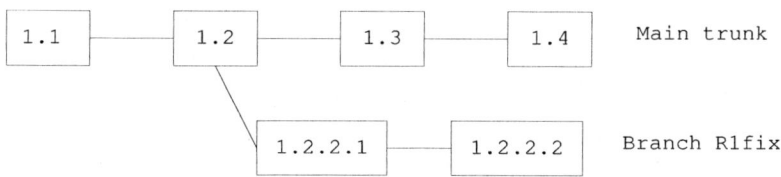

The branch 1.2.2 has been given the tag (symbolic name) 'R1fix'. The following example assumes that the module 'mod' contains only one file, 'm.c'.

```
# Retrieve the latest revision, 1.4
$ cvs checkout mod

# Merge all changes made on the branch,
# i.e. the changes between revision 1.2
# and 1.2.2.2, into your working copy
# of the file.
```

```
$ cvs update -j R1fix m.c
```

```
# Create revision 1.5.
$ cvs commit -m "Included R1fix"
```

A conflict can result from a merge operation. If that happens, you should resolve it before committing the new revision. See Section 10.3 [Conflicts example], page 81.

If your source files contain keywords (see Chapter 12 [Keyword substitution], page 93), you might be getting more conflicts than strictly necessary. See Section 5.10 [Merging and keywords], page 60, for information on how to avoid this.

The **checkout** command also supports the '-j *branch*' flag. The same effect as above could be achieved with this:

```
$ cvs checkout -j R1fix mod
$ cvs commit -m "Included R1fix"
```

5.7 Merging from a branch several times

Continuing our example, the revision tree now looks like this:

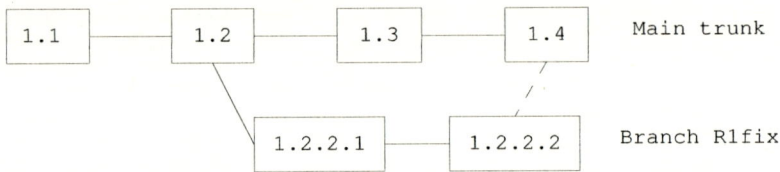

where the dashed line represents the merge from the 'R1fix' branch to the main trunk, as just discussed.

Now suppose that development continues on the 'R1fix' branch:

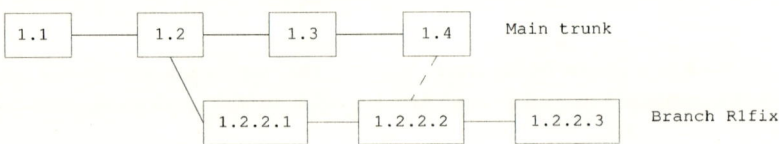

and then you want to merge those new changes onto the main trunk. If you just use the **cvs update -j R1fix m.c** command again, CVS will attempt to merge again the changes which you have already merged, which can have undesirable side effects.

So instead you need to specify that you only want to merge the changes on the branch which have not yet been merged into the trunk. To do that you specify two '-j' options, and CVS merges the changes from the first revision to the second revision. For example, in this case the simplest way would be

```
# Merge changes from 1.2.2.2 to the
# head of the R1fix branch
cvs update -j 1.2.2.2 -j R1fix m.c
```

The problem with this is that you need to specify the 1.2.2.2 revision manually. A slightly better approach might be to use the date the last merge was done:

```
cvs update -j R1fix:yesterday -j R1fix m.c
```

Better yet, tag the R1fix branch after every merge into the trunk, and then use that tag for subsequent merges:

```
cvs update -j merged_from_R1fix_to_trunk -j R1fix m.c
```

5.8 Merging differences between any two revisions

With two '-j *revision*' flags, the update (and checkout) command can merge the differences between any two revisions into your working file.

```
$ cvs update -j 1.5 -j 1.3 backend.c
```

will undo all changes made between revision 1.3 and 1.5. Note the order of the revisions!

If you try to use this option when operating on multiple files, remember that the numeric revisions will probably be very different between the various files. You almost always use symbolic tags rather than revision numbers when operating on multiple files.

Specifying two '-j' options can also undo file removals or additions. For example, suppose you have a file named 'file1' which existed as revision 1.1, and you then removed it (thus adding a dead revision 1.2). Now suppose you want to add it again, with the same contents it had previously. Here is how to do it:

```
$ cvs update -j 1.2 -j 1.1 file1
U file1
$ cvs commit -m test
Checking in file1;
/tmp/cvs-sanity/cvsroot/first-dir/file1,v  <--  file1
new revision: 1.3; previous revision: 1.2
done
$
```

5.9 Merging can add or remove files

If the changes which you are merging involve removing or adding some
files, update -j will reflect such additions or removals.

For example:

```
cvs update -A
touch a b c
cvs add a b c ; cvs ci -m "added" a b c
cvs tag -b branchtag
cvs update -r branchtag
touch d ; cvs add d
rm a ; cvs rm a
cvs ci -m "added d, removed a"
cvs update -A
cvs update -jbranchtag
```

After these commands are executed and a 'cvs commit' is done, file 'a'
will be removed and file 'd' added in the main branch.

5.10 Merging and keywords

If you merge files containing keywords (see Chapter 12 [Keyword substitu-
tion], page 93), you will normally get numerous conflicts during the merge,
because the keywords are expanded differently in the revisions which you
are merging.

Therefore, you will often want to specify the '-kk' (see Section 12.4 [Sub-
stitution modes], page 95) switch to the merge command line. By sub-
stituting just the name of the keyword, not the expanded value of that
keyword, this option ensures that the revisions which you are merging will
be the same as each other, and avoid spurious conflicts.

For example, suppose you have a file like this:

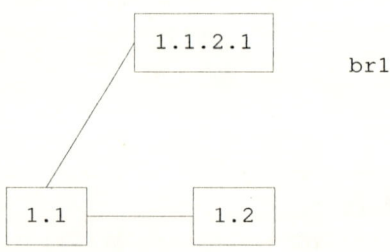

and your working directory is currently on the trunk (revision 1.2). Then
you might get the following results from a merge:

```
$ cat file1
key $Revision: 1.2 $
 . . .
$ cvs update -j br1
U file1
RCS file: /cvsroot/first-dir/file1,v
retrieving revision 1.1
retrieving revision 1.1.2.1
Merging differences between 1.1 and 1.1.2.1 into file1
rcsmerge: warning: conflicts during merge
$ cat file1
<<<<<<< file1
key $Revision: 1.2 $
=======
key $Revision: 1.1.2.1 $
>>>>>>> 1.1.2.1
 . . .
```

What happened was that the merge tried to merge the differences between 1.1 and 1.1.2.1 into your working directory. So, since the keyword changed from Revision: 1.1 to Revision: 1.1.2.1, CVS tried to merge that change into your working directory, which conflicted with the fact that your working directory had contained Revision: 1.2.

Here is what happens if you had used '-kk':

```
$ cat file1
key $Revision: 1.2 $
 . . .
$ cvs update -kk -j br1
U file1
RCS file: /cvsroot/first-dir/file1,v
retrieving revision 1.1
retrieving revision 1.1.2.1
Merging differences between 1.1 and 1.1.2.1 into file1
$ cat file1
key $Revision$
 . . .
```

What is going on here is that revision 1.1 and 1.1.2.1 both expand as plain Revision, and therefore merging the changes between them into the working directory need not change anything. Therefore, there is no conflict.

There is, however, one major caveat with using '-kk' on merges. Namely, it overrides whatever keyword expansion mode CVS would normally have used. In particular, this is a problem if the mode had been '-kb' for a binary file. Therefore, if your repository contains binary files, you will need to deal with the conflicts rather than using '-kk'.

6 Recursive behavior

Almost all of the subcommands of CVS work recursively when you specify a directory as an argument. For instance, consider this directory structure:

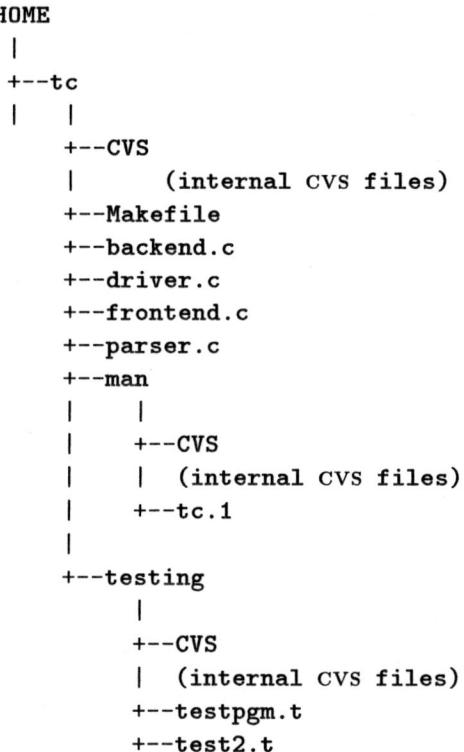

```
$HOME
   |
   +--tc
   |   |
   |   +--CVS
   |   |       (internal CVS files)
   |   +--Makefile
   |   +--backend.c
   |   +--driver.c
   |   +--frontend.c
   |   +--parser.c
   |   +--man
   |   |    |
   |   |    +--CVS
   |   |    |  (internal CVS files)
   |   |    +--tc.1
   |   |
   |   +--testing
   |        |
   |        +--CVS
   |        |  (internal CVS files)
   |        +--testpgm.t
   |        +--test2.t
```

If 'tc' is the current working directory, the following is true:

- 'cvs update testing' is equivalent to

      cvs update testing/testpgm.t testing/test2.t

- 'cvs update testing man' updates all files in the subdirectories

- 'cvs update .' or just 'cvs update' updates all files in the tc directory

If no arguments are given to update it will update all files in the current working directory and all its subdirectories. In other words, '.' is a default argument to update. This is also true for most of the CVS subcommands, not only the update command.

The recursive behavior of the CVS subcommands can be turned off with the '-l' option. Conversely, the '-R' option can be used to force recursion if '-l' is specified in '~/.cvsrc' (see Section A.3 [~/.cvsrc], page 108).

```
$ cvs update -l        # Don't update files in subdirectories
```

7 Adding, removing, and renaming files and directories

In the course of a project, one will often add new files. Likewise with removing or renaming, or with directories. The general concept to keep in mind in all these cases is that instead of making an irreversible change you want CVS to record the fact that a change has taken place, just as with modifying an existing file. The exact mechanisms to do this in CVS vary depending on the situation.

7.1 Adding files to a directory

To add a new file to a directory, follow these steps.

- You must have a working copy of the directory. See Section 1.3.1 [Getting the source], page 6.

- Create the new file inside your working copy of the directory.

- Use 'cvs add *filename*' to tell CVS that you want to version control the file. If the file contains binary data, specify '-kb' (see Chapter 9 [Binary files], page 75).

- Use 'cvs commit *filename*' to actually check in the file into the repository. Other developers cannot see the file until you perform this step.

You can also use the **add** command to add a new directory.

Unlike most other commands, the **add** command is not recursive. You cannot even type 'cvs add foo/bar'! Instead, you have to

```
$ cd foo
$ cvs add bar
```

cvs add [-k *kflag*] [-m *message*] *files* . . .   Command
Schedule *files* to be added to the repository. The files or directories specified with **add** must already exist in the current directory. To add a whole new directory hierarchy to the source repository (for example, files received from a third-party vendor), use the **import** command instead. See Section A.12 [import], page 132.

The added files are not placed in the source repository until you use **commit** to make the change permanent. Doing an **add** on a file that was removed with the **remove** command will undo the effect of the **remove**, unless a **commit** command intervened. See Section 7.2 [Removing files], page 66, for an example.

The '-k' option specifies the default way that this file will be checked out; for more information see Section 12.4 [Substitution modes], page 95.

The '-m' option specifies a description for the file. This description appears in the history log (if it is enabled, see Section C.11 [history file], page 173). It will also be saved in the version history inside the repository when the file is committed. The log command displays this description. The description can be changed using 'admin -t'. See Section A.6 [admin], page 114. If you omit the '-m *description*' flag, an empty string will be used. You will not be prompted for a description.

For example, the following commands add the file 'backend.c' to the repository:

```
$ cvs add backend.c
$ cvs commit -m "Early version." backend.c
```

When you add a file it is added only on the branch which you are working on (see Chapter 5 [Branching and merging], page 53). You can later merge the additions to another branch if you want (see Section 5.9 [Merging adds and removals], page 60).

7.2 Removing files

Directories change. New files are added, and old files disappear. Still, you want to be able to retrieve an exact copy of old releases.

Here is what you can do to remove a file, but remain able to retrieve old revisions:

- Make sure that you have not made any uncommitted modifications to the file. See Section 1.3.4 [Viewing differences], page 9, for one way to do that. You can also use the status or update command. If you remove the file without committing your changes, you will of course not be able to retrieve the file as it was immediately before you deleted it.

- Remove the file from your working copy of the directory. You can for instance use rm.

- Use 'cvs remove *filename*' to tell CVS that you really want to delete the file.

- Use 'cvs commit *filename*' to actually perform the removal of the file from the repository.

When you commit the removal of the file, CVS records the fact that the file no longer exists. It is possible for a file to exist on only some branches and not on others, or to re-add another file with the same name later. CVS will correctly create or not create the file, based on the '-r' and '-D' options specified to **checkout** or **update**.

cvs remove [*options*] *files* ...   Command

Schedule file(s) to be removed from the repository (files which have not already been removed from the working directory are not processed). This command does not actually remove the file from the repository until you commit the removal. For a full list of options, see Appendix B [Invoking CVS], page 145.

Here is an example of removing several files:

```
$ cd test
$ rm *.c
$ cvs remove
cvs remove: Removing .
cvs remove: scheduling a.c for removal
cvs remove: scheduling b.c for removal
cvs remove: use 'cvs commit' to remove these files
permanently
$ cvs ci -m "Removed unneeded files"
cvs commit: Examining .
cvs commit: Committing .
```

As a convenience you can remove the file and **cvs remove** it in one step, by specifying the '-f' option. For example, the above example could also be done like this:

```
$ cd test
$ cvs remove -f *.c
cvs remove: scheduling a.c for removal
cvs remove: scheduling b.c for removal
cvs remove: use 'cvs commit' to remove these files
permanently
$ cvs ci -m "Removed unneeded files"
cvs commit: Examining .
cvs commit: Committing .
```

If you execute **remove** for a file, and then change your mind before you commit, you can undo the **remove** with an **add** command.

```
$ ls
CVS    ja.h  oj.c
$ rm oj.c
$ cvs remove oj.c
cvs remove: scheduling oj.c for removal
```

```
cvs remove: use 'cvs commit' to remove this file
permanently
$ cvs add oj.c
U oj.c
cvs add: oj.c, version 1.1.1.1, resurrected
```

If you realize your mistake before you run the **remove** command you can use **update** to resurrect the file:

```
$ rm oj.c
$ cvs update oj.c
cvs update: warning: oj.c was lost
U oj.c
```

When you remove a file it is removed only on the branch which you are working on (see Chapter 5 [Branching and merging], page 53). You can later merge the removals to another branch if you want (see Section 5.9 [Merging adds and removals], page 60).

7.3 Removing directories

In concept removing directories is somewhat similar to removing files— you want the directory to not exist in your current working directories, but you also want to be able to retrieve old releases in which the directory existed.

The way that you remove a directory is to remove all the files in it. You don't remove the directory itself; there is no way to do that. Instead you specify the '-P' option to **cvs update** or **cvs checkout**, which will cause CVS to remove empty directories from working directories. (Note that **cvs export** always removes empty directories.) Probably the best way to do this is to always specify '-P'; if you want an empty directory then put a dummy file (for example '.keepme') in it to prevent '-P' from removing it.

Note that '-P' is implied by the '-r' or '-D' options of **checkout**. This way CVS will be able to correctly create the directory or not depending on whether the particular version you are checking out contains any files in that directory.

7.4 Moving and renaming files

Moving files to a different directory or renaming them is not difficult, but some of the ways in which this works may be non-obvious. (Moving or renaming a directory is even harder. See Section 7.5 [Moving directories], page 70.).

The examples below assume that the file *old* is renamed to *new*.

7.4.1 The Normal way to Rename

The normal way to move a file is to copy *old* to *new*, and then issue the normal CVS commands to remove *old* from the repository, and add *new* to it.

```
$ mv old new
$ cvs remove old
$ cvs add new
$ cvs commit -m "Renamed old to new" old new
```

This is the simplest way to move a file, it is not error-prone, and it preserves the history of what was done. Note that to access the history of the file you must specify the old or the new name, depending on what portion of the history you are accessing. For example, cvs log *old* will give the log up until the time of the rename.

When *new* is committed its revision numbers will start again, usually at 1.1, so if that bothers you, use the '-r rev' option to commit. For more information see Section 4.3 [Assigning revisions], page 43.

7.4.2 Moving the history file

This method is more dangerous, since it involves moving files inside the repository. Read this entire section before trying it out!

```
$ cd $CVSROOT/dir
$ mv old,v new,v
```

Advantages:

- The log of changes is maintained intact.
- The revision numbers are not affected.

Disadvantages:

- Old releases cannot easily be fetched from the repository. (The file will show up as *new* even in revisions from the time before it was renamed).
- There is no log information of when the file was renamed.
- Nasty things might happen if someone accesses the history file while you are moving it. Make sure no one else runs any of the CVS commands while you move it.

7.4.3 Copying the history file

This way also involves direct modifications to the repository. It is safe, but not without drawbacks.

```
# Copy the RCS file inside the repository
$ cd $CVSROOT/dir
$ cp old,v new,v
# Remove the old file
$ cd ~/dir
$ rm old
$ cvs remove old
$ cvs commit old
# Remove all tags from new
$ cvs update new
$ cvs log new      # Remember the non-branch tag names
$ cvs tag -d tag1 new
$ cvs tag -d tag2 new
...
```

By removing the tags you will be able to check out old revisions.

Advantages:

- Checking out old revisions works correctly, as long as you use '-r *tag*' and not '-D *date*' to retrieve the revisions.
- The log of changes is maintained intact.
- The revision numbers are not affected.

Disadvantages:

- You cannot easily see the history of the file across the rename.

7.5 Moving and renaming directories

The normal way to rename or move a directory is to rename or move each file within it as described in Section 7.4.1 [Outside], page 69. Then check out with the '-P' option, as described in Section 7.3 [Removing directories], page 68.

If you really want to hack the repository to rename or delete a directory in the repository, you can do it like this:

1. Inform everyone who has a checked out copy of the directory that the directory will be renamed. They should commit all their changes, and remove their working copies, before you take the steps below.

2. Rename the directory inside the repository.

   ```
   $ cd $CVSROOT/parent-dir
   $ mv old-dir new-dir
   ```

3. Fix the CVS administrative files, if necessary (for instance if you renamed an entire module).

4. Tell everyone that they can check out again and continue working.

If someone had a working copy the CVS commands will cease to work for him, until he removes the directory that disappeared inside the repository.

It is almost always better to move the files in the directory instead of moving the directory. If you move the directory you are unlikely to be able to retrieve old releases correctly, since they probably depend on the name of the directories.

8 History browsing

Once you have used CVS to store a version control history—what files have changed when, how, and by whom, there are a variety of mechanisms for looking through the history.

8.1 Log messages

Whenever you commit a file you specify a log message.

To look through the log messages which have been specified for every revision which has been committed, use the **cvs log** command (see Section A.13 [log], page 134).

8.2 The history database

You can use the history file (see Section C.11 [history file], page 173) to log various CVS actions. To retrieve the information from the history file, use the **cvs history** command (see Section A.11 [history], page 129).

Note: you can control what is logged to this file by using the 'LogHistory' keyword in the 'CVSROOT/config' file (see Section C.13 [config], page 174).

8.3 User-defined logging

You can customize CVS to log various kinds of actions, in whatever manner you choose. These mechanisms operate by executing a script at various times. The script might append a message to a file listing the information and the programmer who created it, or send mail to a group of developers, or, perhaps, post a message to a particular newsgroup. To log commits, use the 'loginfo' file (see Section C.7 [loginfo], page 169). To log commits, checkouts, exports, and tags, respectively, you can also use the '-i', '-o', '-e', and '-t' options in the modules file. For a more flexible way of giving notifications to various users, which requires less in the way of keeping centralized scripts up to date, use the **cvs watch add** command (see Section 10.6.2 [Getting Notified], page 86); this command is useful even if you are not using **cvs watch on**.

The 'taginfo' file defines programs to execute when someone executes a **tag** or **rtag** command. The 'taginfo' file has the standard form for administrative files (see Appendix C [Administrative files], page 159), where each line is a regular expression followed by a command to execute. The arguments passed to the command are, in order, the *tagname*, *operation* (**add** for **tag**, **mov** for **tag -F**, and **del** for **tag -d**), *repository*, and any

remaining are pairs of *filename revision*. A non-zero exit of the filter
program will cause the tag to be aborted.

Here is an example of using taginfo to log tag and rtag commands. In the
taginfo file put:

    ALL /usr/local/cvsroot/CVSROOT/loggit

Where '/usr/local/cvsroot/CVSROOT/loggit' contains the following
script:

    #!/bin/sh
    echo "$@" >>/home/kingdon/cvsroot/CVSROOT/taglog

8.4 Annotate command

cvs annotate [-flR] [-r rev | -D date] *files* ...   Command
    For each file in *files*, print the head revision of the trunk, together with
    information on the last modification for each line. For example:

    $ cvs annotate ssfile
    Annotations for ssfile
    ****
    1.1   (mary   27-Mar-96): ssfile line 1
    1.2   (joe   28-Mar-96): ssfile line 2

    The file 'ssfile' currently contains two lines. The ssfile line 1 line
    was checked in by mary on March 27. Then, on March 28, joe added a
    line ssfile line 2, without modifying the ssfile line 1 line. This
    report doesn't tell you anything about lines which have been deleted
    or replaced; you need to use cvs diff for that (see Section A.9 [diff],
    page 126).

The options to cvs annotate are listed in Appendix B [Invoking CVS],
page 145, and can be used to select the files and revisions to annotate.
The options are described in more detail in Section A.5 [Common options],
page 111.

9 Handling binary files

The most common use for CVS is to store text files. With text files, CVS can merge revisions, display the differences between revisions in a human-visible fashion, and other such operations. However, if you are willing to give up a few of these abilities, CVS can store binary files. For example, one might store a web site in CVS including both text files and binary images.

9.1 The issues with binary files

While the need to manage binary files may seem obvious if the files that you customarily work with are binary, putting them into version control does present some additional issues.

One basic function of version control is to show the differences between two revisions. For example, if someone else checked in a new version of a file, you may wish to look at what they changed and determine whether their changes are good. For text files, CVS provides this functionality via the `cvs diff` command. For binary files, it may be possible to extract the two revisions and then compare them with a tool external to CVS (for example, word processing software often has such a feature). If there is no such tool, one must track changes via other mechanisms, such as urging people to write good log messages, and hoping that the changes they actually made were the changes that they intended to make.

Another ability of a version control system is the ability to merge two revisions. For CVS this happens in two contexts. The first is when users make changes in separate working directories (see Chapter 10 [Multiple developers], page 79). The second is when one merges explicitly with the 'update -j' command (see Chapter 5 [Branching and merging], page 53).

In the case of text files, CVS can merge changes made independently, and signal a conflict if the changes conflict. With binary files, the best that CVS can do is present the two different copies of the file, and leave it to the user to resolve the conflict. The user may choose one copy or the other, or may run an external merge tool which knows about that particular file format, if one exists. Note that having the user merge relies primarily on the user to not accidentally omit some changes, and thus is potentially error prone.

If this process is thought to be undesirable, the best choice may be to avoid merging. To avoid the merges that result from separate working directories, see the discussion of reserved checkouts (file locking) in Chapter 10 [Multiple developers], page 79. To avoid the merges resulting from branches, restrict use of branches.

9.2 How to store binary files

There are two issues with using CVS to store binary files. The first is that CVS by default converts line endings between the canonical form in which they are stored in the repository (linefeed only), and the form appropriate to the operating system in use on the client (for example, carriage return followed by line feed for Windows NT).

The second is that a binary file might happen to contain data which looks like a keyword (see Chapter 12 [Keyword substitution], page 93), so keyword expansion must be turned off.

The '-kb' option available with some CVS commands insures that neither line ending conversion nor keyword expansion will be done.

Here is an example of how you can create a new file using the '-kb' flag:

```
$ echo '$Id$' > kotest
$ cvs add -kb -m"A test file" kotest
$ cvs ci -m"First checkin; contains a keyword" kotest
```

If a file accidentally gets added without '-kb', one can use the cvs admin command to recover. For example:

```
$ echo '$Id$' > kotest
$ cvs add -m"A test file" kotest
$ cvs ci -m"First checkin; contains a keyword" kotest
$ cvs admin -kb kotest
$ cvs update -A kotest
# For non-unix systems:
# Copy in a good copy of the file from outside CVS
$ cvs commit -m "make it binary" kotest
```

When you check in the file 'kotest' the file is not preserved as a binary file, because you did not check it in as a binary file. The cvs admin -kb command sets the default keyword substitution method for this file, but it does not alter the working copy of the file that you have. If you need to cope with line endings (that is, you are using CVS on a non-unix system), then you need to check in a new copy of the file, as shown by the cvs commit command above. On unix, the cvs update -A command suffices.

However, in using cvs admin -k to change the keyword expansion, be aware that the keyword expansion mode is not version controlled. This means that, for example, that if you have a text file in old releases, and a binary file with the same name in new releases, CVS provides no way to check out the file in text or binary mode depending on what version you are checking out. There is no good workaround for this problem.

You can also set a default for whether cvs add and cvs import treat a file as binary based on its name; for example you could say that files who names end in '`.exe`' are binary. See Section C.2 [Wrappers], page 163. There is currently no way to have CVS detect whether a file is binary based on its contents. The main difficulty with designing such a feature is that it is not clear how to distinguish between binary and non-binary files, and the rules to apply would vary considerably with the operating system.

10 Multiple developers

When more than one person works on a software project things often get complicated. Often, two people try to edit the same file simultaneously. One solution, known as *file locking* or *reserved checkouts*, is to allow only one person to edit each file at a time. This is the only solution with some version control systems, including RCS and SCCS. Currently the usual way to get reserved checkouts with CVS is the `cvs admin -l` command (see Section A.6.1 [admin options], page 115). This is not as nicely integrated into CVS as the watch features, described below, but it seems that most people with a need for reserved checkouts find it adequate. It also may be possible to use the watches features described below, together with suitable procedures (not enforced by software), to avoid having two people edit at the same time.

The default model with CVS is known as *unreserved checkouts*. In this model, developers can edit their own *working copy* of a file simultaneously. The first person that commits his changes has no automatic way of knowing that another has started to edit it. Others will get an error message when they try to commit the file. They must then use CVS commands to bring their working copy up to date with the repository revision. This process is almost automatic.

CVS also supports mechanisms which facilitate various kinds of communication, without actually enforcing rules like reserved checkouts do.

The rest of this chapter describes how these various models work, and some of the issues involved in choosing between them.

10.1 File status

Based on what operations you have performed on a checked out file, and what operations others have performed to that file in the repository, one can classify a file in a number of states. The states, as reported by the `status` command, are:

Up-to-date   The file is identical with the latest revision in the repository
             for the branch in use.

Locally Modified
             You have edited the file, and not yet committed your
             changes.

Locally Added
             You have added the file with **add**, and not yet committed
             your changes.

Locally Removed

> You have removed the file with **remove**, and not yet committed your changes.

Needs Checkout

> Someone else has committed a newer revision to the repository. The name is slightly misleading; you will ordinarily use **update** rather than **checkout** to get that newer revision.

Needs Patch

> Like Needs Checkout, but the CVS server will send a patch rather than the entire file. Sending a patch or sending an entire file accomplishes the same thing.

Needs Merge

> Someone else has committed a newer revision to the repository, and you have also made modifications to the file.

File had conflicts on merge

> This is like Locally Modified, except that a previous **update** command gave a conflict. If you have not already done so, you need to resolve the conflict as described in Section 10.3 [Conflicts example], page 81.

Unknown   CVS doesn't know anything about this file. For example, you have created a new file and have not run **add**.

To help clarify the file status, **status** also reports the Working revision which is the revision that the file in the working directory derives from, and the Repository revision which is the latest revision in the repository for the branch in use.

The options to **status** are listed in Appendix B [Invoking CVS], page 145. For information on its Sticky tag and Sticky date output, see Section 4.9 [Sticky tags], page 50. For information on its Sticky options output, see the '-k' option in Section A.16.1 [update options], page 140.

You can think of the **status** and **update** commands as somewhat complementary. You use **update** to bring your files up to date, and you can use **status** to give you some idea of what an **update** would do (of course, the state of the repository might change before you actually run **update**). In fact, if you want a command to display file status in a more brief format than is displayed by the **status** command, you can invoke

    $ cvs -n -q update

The '-n' option means to not actually do the update, but merely to display statuses; the '-q' option avoids printing the name of each directory. For more information on the **update** command, and these options, see Appendix B [Invoking CVS], page 145.

10.2 Bringing a file up to date

When you want to update or merge a file, use the **update** command. For files that are not up to date this is roughly equivalent to a **checkout** command: the newest revision of the file is extracted from the repository and put in your working directory.

Your modifications to a file are never lost when you use **update**. If no newer revision exists, running **update** has no effect. If you have edited the file, and a newer revision is available, CVS will merge all changes into your working copy.

For instance, imagine that you checked out revision 1.4 and started editing it. In the meantime someone else committed revision 1.5, and shortly after that revision 1.6. If you run **update** on the file now, CVS will incorporate all changes between revision 1.4 and 1.6 into your file.

If any of the changes between 1.4 and 1.6 were made too close to any of the changes you have made, an *overlap* occurs. In such cases a warning is printed, and the resulting file includes both versions of the lines that overlap, delimited by special markers. See Section A.16 [update], page 140, for a complete description of the **update** command.

10.3 Conflicts example

Suppose revision 1.4 of 'driver.c' contains this:

```
#include <stdio.h>

void main()
{
    parse();
    if (nerr == 0)
        gencode();
    else
        fprintf(stderr, "No code generated.\n");
    exit(nerr == 0 ? 0 : 1);
}
```

Revision 1.6 of 'driver.c' contains this:

```
#include <stdio.h>

int main(int argc,
         char **argv)
{
    parse();
```

```
    if (argc != 1)
    {
        fprintf(stderr, "tc: No args expected.\n");
        exit(1);
    }
    if (nerr == 0)
        gencode();
    else
        fprintf(stderr, "No code generated.\n");
    exit(!!nerr);
}
```

Your working copy of 'driver.c', based on revision 1.4, contains this before you run 'cvs update':

```
#include <stdlib.h>
#include <stdio.h>

void main()
{
    init_scanner();
    parse();
    if (nerr == 0)
        gencode();
    else
        fprintf(stderr, "No code generated.\n");
    exit(nerr == 0 ? EXIT_SUCCESS : EXIT_FAILURE);
}
```

You run 'cvs update':

```
$ cvs update driver.c
RCS file: /usr/local/cvsroot/yoyodyne/tc/driver.c,v
retrieving revision 1.4
retrieving revision 1.6
Merging differences between 1.4 and 1.6 into driver.c
rcsmerge warning: overlaps during merge
cvs update: conflicts found in driver.c
C driver.c
```

CVS tells you that there were some conflicts. Your original working file is saved unmodified in '.#driver.c.1.4'. The new version of 'driver.c' contains this:

```
#include <stdlib.h>
#include <stdio.h>
```

```
int main(int argc,
         char **argv)
{
    init_scanner();
    parse();
    if (argc != 1)
    {
        fprintf(stderr, "tc: No args expected.\n");
        exit(1);
    }
    if (nerr == 0)
        gencode();
    else
        fprintf(stderr, "No code generated.\n");
<<<<<<< driver.c
    exit(nerr == 0 ? EXIT_SUCCESS : EXIT_FAILURE);
=======
    exit(!!nerr);
>>>>>>> 1.6
}
```

Note how all non-overlapping modifications are incorporated in your working copy, and that the overlapping section is clearly marked with '<<<<<<<', '=======' and '>>>>>>>'.

You resolve the conflict by editing the file, removing the markers and the erroneous line. Suppose you end up with this file:

```
#include <stdlib.h>
#include <stdio.h>

int main(int argc,
         char **argv)
{
    init_scanner();
    parse();
    if (argc != 1)
    {
        fprintf(stderr, "tc: No args expected.\n");
        exit(1);
    }
    if (nerr == 0)
        gencode();
```

```
        else
            fprintf(stderr, "No code generated.\n");
        exit(nerr == 0 ? EXIT_SUCCESS : EXIT_FAILURE);
    }
```

You can now go ahead and commit this as revision 1.7.

```
    $ cvs commit -m "Initialize scanner.
        Use symbolic exit values." driver.c
    Checking in driver.c;
    /usr/local/cvsroot/yoyodyne/tc/driver.c,v  <--  driver.c
    new revision: 1.7; previous revision: 1.6
    done
```

For your protection, CVS will refuse to check in a file if a conflict occurred and you have not resolved the conflict. Currently to resolve a conflict, you must change the timestamp on the file. In previous versions of CVS, you also needed to insure that the file contains no conflict markers. Because your file may legitimately contain conflict markers (that is, occurrences of '>>>>>>> ' at the start of a line that don't mark a conflict), the current version of CVS will print a warning and proceed to check in the file.

If you use release 1.04 or later of pcl-cvs (a GNU Emacs front-end for CVS) you can use an Emacs package called emerge to help you resolve conflicts. See the documentation for pcl-cvs.

10.4 Informing others about commits

It is often useful to inform others when you commit a new revision of a file. The '-i' option of the 'modules' file, or the 'loginfo' file, can be used to automate this process. See Section C.1 [modules], page 159. See Section C.7 [loginfo], page 169. You can use these features of CVS to, for instance, instruct CVS to mail a message to all developers, or post a message to a local newsgroup.

10.5 Several developers simultaneously attempting to run CVS

If several developers try to run CVS at the same time, one may get the following message:

```
    [11:43:23] waiting for bach's lock in /usr/local/cvsroot/foo
```

CVS will try again every 30 seconds, and either continue with the operation or print the message again, if it still needs to wait. If a lock seems to stick around for an undue amount of time, find the person holding the lock and ask them about the cvs command they are running. If they aren't running a cvs command, look in the repository directory mentioned in the message and remove files which they own whose names start with '#cvs.rfl', '#cvs.wfl', or '#cvs.lock'.

Note that these locks are to protect CVS's internal data structures and have no relationship to the word *lock* in the sense used by RCS— which refers to reserved checkouts (see Chapter 10 [Multiple developers], page 79).

Any number of people can be reading from a given repository at a time; only when someone is writing do the locks prevent other people from reading or writing.

One might hope for the following property

> If someone commits some changes in one cvs command, then an update by someone else will either get all the changes, or none of them.

but CVS does *not* have this property. For example, given the files

    a/one.c
    a/two.c
    b/three.c
    b/four.c

if someone runs

    cvs ci a/two.c b/three.c

and someone else runs `cvs update` at the same time, the person running update might get only the change to 'b/three.c' and not the change to 'a/two.c'.

10.6 Mechanisms to track who is editing files

For many groups, use of CVS in its default mode is perfectly satisfactory. Users may sometimes go to check in a modification only to find that another modification has intervened, but they deal with it and proceed with their check in. Other groups prefer to be able to know who is editing what files, so that if two people try to edit the same file they can choose to talk about who is doing what when rather than be surprised at check in time. The features in this section allow such coordination, while retaining the ability of two developers to edit the same file at the same time.

For maximum benefit developers should use `cvs edit` (not chmod) to make files read-write to edit them, and `cvs release` (not rm) to discard a working directory which is no longer in use, but CVS is not able to enforce this behavior.

10.6.1 Telling CVS to watch certain files

To enable the watch features, you first specify that certain files are to be watched.

cvs watch on [-1R] *files* . . .   Command
> Specify that developers should run **cvs edit** before editing *files*. CVS will create working copies of *files* read-only, to remind developers to run the **cvs edit** command before working on them.
>
> If *files* includes the name of a directory, CVS arranges to watch all files added to the corresponding repository directory, and sets a default for files added in the future; this allows the user to set notification policies on a per-directory basis. The contents of the directory are processed recursively, unless the -1 option is given. The -R option can be used to force recursion if the -1 option is set in '~/.cvsrc' (see Section A.3 [~/.cvsrc], page 108).
>
> If *files* is omitted, it defaults to the current directory.

cvs watch off [-1R] *files* . . .   Command
> Do not create *files* read-only on checkout; thus, developers will not be reminded to use **cvs edit** and **cvs unedit**.
>
> The *files* and options are processed as for **cvs watch on**.

10.6.2 Telling CVS to notify you

You can tell CVS that you want to receive notifications about various actions taken on a file. You can do this without using **cvs watch on** for the file, but generally you will want to use **cvs watch on**, so that developers use the **cvs edit** command.

cvs watch add [-a *action*] [-1R] *files* . . .   Command
> Add the current user to the list of people to receive notification of work done on *files*.
>
> The -a option specifies what kinds of events CVS should notify the user about. *action* is one of the following:

> edit   Another user has applied the **cvs edit** command (described below) to a file.

> unedit   Another user has applied the **cvs unedit** command (described below) or the **cvs release** command to a file, or has deleted the file and allowed **cvs update** to recreate it.

commit   Another user has committed changes to a file.

all   All of the above.

none   None of the above. (This is useful with cvs edit, de-
            scribed below.)

The -a option may appear more than once, or not at all. If omitted,
the action defaults to all.

The *files* and options are processed as for the cvs watch commands.

cvs watch remove [-a *action*] [-1R] *files* . . .   Command
    Remove a notification request established using cvs watch add; the
    arguments are the same. If the -a option is present, only watches for
    the specified actions are removed.

When the conditions exist for notification, CVS calls the 'notify' administrative file. Edit 'notify' as one edits the other administrative files (see
Section 2.4 [Intro administrative files], page 23). This file follows the usual
conventions for administrative files (see Section C.3.1 [syntax], page 165),
where each line is a regular expression followed by a command to execute. The command should contain a single occurrence of '%s' which will
be replaced by the user to notify; the rest of the information regarding
the notification will be supplied to the command on standard input. The
standard thing to put in the notify file is the single line:

    ALL mail %s -s "CVS notification"

This causes users to be notified by electronic mail.

Note that if you set this up in the straightforward way, users receive
notifications on the server machine. One could of course write a 'notify'
script which directed notifications elsewhere, but to make this easy, CVS
allows you to associate a notification address for each user. To do so
create a file 'users' in 'CVSROOT' with a line for each user in the format
user:value. Then instead of passing the name of the user to be notified
to 'notify', CVS will pass the *value* (normally an email address on some
other machine).

CVS does not notify you for your own changes. Currently this check is
done based on whether the user name of the person taking the action
which triggers notification matches the user name of the person getting
notification. In fact, in general, the watches features only track one edit
by each user. It probably would be more useful if watches tracked each
working directory separately, so this behavior might be worth changing.

10.6.3 How to edit a file which is being watched

Since a file which is being watched is checked out read-only, you cannot simply edit it. To make it read-write, and inform others that you are planning to edit it, use the **cvs edit** command. Some systems call this a *checkout*, but CVS uses that term for obtaining a copy of the sources (see Section 1.3.1 [Getting the source], page 6), an operation which those systems call a *get* or a *fetch*.

---

cvs edit [*options*] *files . . .*   Command

Prepare to edit the working files *files*. CVS makes the *files* read-write, and notifies users who have requested **edit** notification for any of *files*.

The **cvs edit** command accepts the same *options* as the **cvs watch add** command, and establishes a temporary watch for the user on *files*; CVS will remove the watch when *files* are **unedited** or **committed**. If the user does not wish to receive notifications, she should specify **-a none**.

The *files* and options are processed as for the **cvs watch** commands.

Normally when you are done with a set of changes, you use the **cvs commit** command, which checks in your changes and returns the watched files to their usual read-only state. But if you instead decide to abandon your changes, or not to make any changes, you can use the **cvs unedit** command.

---

cvs unedit [-1R] *files . . .*   Command

Abandon work on the working files *files*, and revert them to the repository versions on which they are based. CVS makes those *files* read-only for which users have requested notification using **cvs watch on**. CVS notifies users who have requested **unedit** notification for any of *files*.

The *files* and options are processed as for the **cvs watch** commands.

If watches are not in use, the **unedit** command probably does not work, and the way to revert to the repository version is to remove the file and then use **cvs update** to get a new copy. The meaning is not precisely the same; removing and updating may also bring in some changes which have been made in the repository since the last time you updated.

When using client/server CVS, you can use the **cvs edit** and **cvs unedit** commands even if CVS is unable to successfully communicate with the server; the notifications will be sent upon the next successful CVS command.

10.6.4 Information about who is watching and editing

cvs watchers [-1R] *files* . . .   Command
> List the users currently watching changes to *files*. The report includes the files being watched, and the mail address of each watcher.
>
> The *files* and options are processed as for the **cvs watch** commands.

cvs editors [-1R] *files* . . .   Command
> List the users currently working on *files*. The report includes the mail address of each user, the time when the user began working with the file, and the host and path of the working directory containing the file.
>
> The *files* and options are processed as for the **cvs watch** commands.

10.6.5 Using watches with old versions of CVS

If you use the watch features on a repository, it creates 'CVS' directories in the repository and stores the information about watches in that directory. If you attempt to use CVS 1.6 or earlier with the repository, you get an error message such as the following (all on one line):

```
cvs update: cannot open CVS/Entries for reading:
No such file or directory
```

and your operation will likely be aborted. To use the watch features, you must upgrade all copies of CVS which use that repository in local or server mode. If you cannot upgrade, use the **watch off** and **watch remove** commands to remove all watches, and that will restore the repository to a state which CVS 1.6 can cope with.

10.7 Choosing between reserved or unreserved checkouts

Reserved and unreserved checkouts each have pros and cons. Let it be said that a lot of this is a matter of opinion or what works given different groups' working styles, but here is a brief description of some of the issues. There are many ways to organize a team of developers. CVS does not try to enforce a certain organization. It is a tool that can be used in several ways.

Reserved checkouts can be very counter-productive. If two persons want to edit different parts of a file, there may be no reason to prevent either of them from doing so. Also, it is common for someone to take out a lock on a file, because they are planning to edit it, but then forget to release the lock.

People, especially people who are familiar with reserved checkouts, often wonder how often conflicts occur if unreserved checkouts are used, and how difficult they are to resolve. The experience with many groups is that they occur rarely and usually are relatively straightforward to resolve.

The rarity of serious conflicts may be surprising, until one realizes that they occur only when two developers disagree on the proper design for a given section of code; such a disagreement suggests that the team has not been communicating properly in the first place. In order to collaborate under *any* source management regimen, developers must agree on the general design of the system; given this agreement, overlapping changes are usually straightforward to merge.

In some cases unreserved checkouts are clearly inappropriate. If no merge tool exists for the kind of file you are managing (for example word processor files or files edited by Computer Aided Design programs), and it is not desirable to change to a program which uses a mergeable data format, then resolving conflicts is going to be unpleasant enough that you generally will be better off to simply avoid the conflicts instead, by using reserved checkouts.

The watches features described above in Section 10.6 [Watches], page 85 can be considered to be an intermediate model between reserved checkouts and unreserved checkouts. When you go to edit a file, it is possible to find out who else is editing it. And rather than having the system simply forbid both people editing the file, it can tell you what the situation is and let you figure out whether it is a problem in that particular case or not. Therefore, for some groups it can be considered the best of both the reserved checkout and unreserved checkout worlds.

11 Revision management

If you have read this far, you probably have a pretty good grasp on what CVS can do for you. This chapter talks a little about things that you still have to decide.

If you are doing development on your own using CVS you could probably skip this chapter. The questions this chapter takes up become more important when more than one person is working in a repository.

11.1 When to commit?

Your group should decide which policy to use regarding commits. Several policies are possible, and as your experience with CVS grows you will probably find out what works for you.

If you commit files too quickly you might commit files that do not even compile. If your partner updates his working sources to include your buggy file, he will be unable to compile the code. On the other hand, other persons will not be able to benefit from the improvements you make to the code if you commit very seldom, and conflicts will probably be more common.

It is common to only commit files after making sure that they can be compiled. Some sites require that the files pass a test suite. Policies like this can be enforced using the commitinfo file (see Section C.4 [commitinfo], page 165), but you should think twice before you enforce such a convention. By making the development environment too controlled it might become too regimented and thus counter-productive to the real goal, which is to get software written.

12 Keyword substitution

As long as you edit source files inside a working directory you can always find out the state of your files via 'cvs status' and 'cvs log'. But as soon as you export the files from your development environment it becomes harder to identify which revisions they are.

CVS can use a mechanism known as *keyword substitution* (or *keyword expansion*) to help identifying the files. Embedded strings of the form $keyword$ and $keyword:...$ in a file are replaced with strings of the form $keyword:value$ whenever you obtain a new revision of the file.

12.1 Keyword List

This is a list of the keywords:

$Author$ The login name of the user who checked in the revision.

$Date$ The date and time (UTC) the revision was checked in.

$Header$ A standard header containing the full pathname of the RCS file, the revision number, the date (UTC), the author, the state, and the locker (if locked). Files will normally never be locked when you use CVS.

Id Same as $Header$, except that the RCS filename is without a path.

$Name$ Tag name used to check out this file. The keyword is expanded only if one checks out with an explicit tag name. For example, when running the command cvs co -r first, the keyword expands to 'Name: first'.

$Locker$ The login name of the user who locked the revision (empty if not locked, which is the normal case unless cvs admin -l is in use).

Log The log message supplied during commit, preceded by a header containing the RCS filename, the revision number, the author, and the date (UTC). Existing log messages are *not* replaced. Instead, the new log message is inserted after $Log:...$. Each new line is prefixed with the same string which precedes the $Log keyword. For example, if the file contains

```
/* Here is what people have been up to:
 *
 * $Log: frob.c,v $
```

```
* Revision 1.1  1997/01/03 14:23:51  joe
* Add the superfrobnicate option
*
*/
```

then additional lines which are added when expanding the
$Log keyword will be preceded by ' * '. Unlike previous ver-
sions of CVS and RCS, the *comment leader* from the RCS file
is not used. The $Log keyword is useful for accumulating
a complete change log in a source file, but for several reasons it can be problematic. See Section 12.5 [Log keyword],
page 96.

$RCSfile$ The name of the RCS file without a path.

$Revision$

            The revision number assigned to the revision.

$Source$ The full pathname of the RCS file.

$State$ The state assigned to the revision.   States can be as-
            signed with cvs admin -s—see Section A.6.1 [admin op-
            tions], page 115.

12.2 Using keywords

To include a keyword string you simply include the relevant text string,
such as Id, inside the file, and commit the file. CVS will automatically
expand the string as part of the commit operation.

It is common to embed the Id string in the source files so that it gets
passed through to generated files. For example, if you are managing computer program source code, you might include a variable which is initialized to contain that string. Or some C compilers may provide a #pragma
ident directive. Or a document management system might provide a way
to pass a string through to generated files.

The ident command (which is part of the RCS package) can be used to
extract keywords and their values from a file. This can be handy for text
files, but it is even more useful for extracting keywords from binary files.

```
$ ident samp.c
samp.c:
     $Id: samp.c,v 1.5 1993/10/19 14:57:32 ceder Exp $
$ gcc samp.c
$ ident a.out
a.out:
     $Id: samp.c,v 1.5 1993/10/19 14:57:32 ceder Exp $
```

Sccs is another popular revision control system. It has a command, what, which is very similar to ident and used for the same purpose. Many sites without RCS have SCCS. Since what looks for the character sequence @(#) it is easy to include keywords that are detected by either command. Simply prefix the keyword with the magic SCCS phrase, like this:

```
static char *id = "@(#) $Id: ab.c,v 1.5 1993/10/19
    14:57:32 ceder Exp $";
```

12.3 Avoiding substitution

Keyword substitution has its disadvantages. Sometimes you might want the literal text string '$Author$' to appear inside a file without CVS interpreting it as a keyword and expanding it into something like '$Author: ceder $'.

There is unfortunately no way to selectively turn off keyword substitution. You can use '-ko' (see Section 12.4 [Substitution modes], page 95) to turn off keyword substitution entirely.

In many cases you can avoid using keywords in the source, even though they appear in the final product. For example, the source for this manual contains '$@asis{}Author$' whenever the text '$Author$' should appear. In nroff and troff you can embed the null-character \& inside the keyword for a similar effect.

12.4 Substitution modes

Each file has a stored default substitution mode, and each working directory copy of a file also has a substitution mode. The former is set by the '-k' option to cvs add and cvs admin; the latter is set by the '-k' or '-A' options to cvs checkout or cvs update. cvs diff also has a '-k' option. For some examples, see Chapter 9 [Binary files], page 75, and Section 5.10 [Merging and keywords], page 60.

The modes available are:

'-kkv'   Generate keyword strings using the default form, e.g. $Revision: 5.7 $ for the Revision keyword.

'-kkvl'   Like '-kkv', except that a locker's name is always inserted if the given revision is currently locked. The locker's name is only relevant if cvs admin -l is in use.

'-kk'   Generate only keyword names in keyword strings; omit their values. For example, for the Revision keyword, generate the string $Revision$ instead of $Revision: 5.7 $. This

option is useful to ignore differences due to keyword substitution when comparing different revisions of a file (see
Section 5.10 [Merging and keywords], page 60).

'-ko'   Generate the old keyword string, present in the working file
                 just before it was checked in. For example, for the `Revision`
                 keyword, generate the string `$Revision: 1.1 $` instead of
                 `$Revision: 5.7 $` if that is how the string appeared when
                 the file was checked in.

'-kb'   Like '-ko', but also inhibit conversion of line endings between
                 the canonical form in which they are stored in the repository
                 (linefeed only), and the form appropriate to the operating
                 system in use on the client. For systems, like unix, which
                 use linefeed only to terminate lines, this is the same as '-ko'.
                 For more information on binary files, see Chapter 9 [Binary
                 files], page 75.

'-kv'   Generate only keyword values for keyword strings. For ex-
                 ample, for the `Revision` keyword, generate the string `5.7`
                 instead of `$Revision: 5.7 $`. This can help generate files in
                 programming languages where it is hard to strip keyword de-
                 limiters like `$Revision: $` from a string. However, further
                 keyword substitution cannot be performed once the keyword
                 names are removed, so this option should be used with care.

                 One often would like to use '-kv' with **cvs export**—see Sec-
                 tion A.10 [export], page 128. But be aware that doesn't
                 handle an export containing binary files correctly.

12.5 Problems with the Log keyword.

The Log keyword is somewhat controversial. As long as you are working
on your development system the information is easily accessible even if
you do not use the Log keyword—just do a **cvs log**. Once you export
the file the history information might be useless anyhow.

A more serious concern is that CVS is not good at handling Log entries
when a branch is merged onto the main trunk. Conflicts often result from
the merging operation.

People also tend to "fix" the log entries in the file (correcting spelling
mistakes and maybe even factual errors). If that is done the information
from **cvs log** will not be consistent with the information inside the file.
This may or may not be a problem in real life.

It has been suggested that the Log keyword should be inserted *last* in
the file, and not in the files header, if it is to be used at all. That way

the long list of change messages will not interfere with everyday source
file browsing.

13 Tracking third-party sources

If you modify a program to better fit your site, you probably want to include your modifications when the next release of the program arrives. CVS can help you with this task.

In the terminology used in CVS, the supplier of the program is called a *vendor*. The unmodified distribution from the vendor is checked in on its own branch, the *vendor branch*. CVS reserves branch 1.1.1 for this use.

When you modify the source and commit it, your revision will end up on the main trunk. When a new release is made by the vendor, you commit it on the vendor branch and copy the modifications onto the main trunk.

Use the `import` command to create and update the vendor branch. When you import a new file, the vendor branch is made the 'head' revision, so anyone that checks out a copy of the file gets that revision. When a local modification is committed it is placed on the main trunk, and made the 'head' revision.

13.1 Importing for the first time

Use the `import` command to check in the sources for the first time. When you use the `import` command to track third-party sources, the *vendor tag* and *release tags* are useful. The *vendor tag* is a symbolic name for the branch (which is always 1.1.1, unless you use the '-b *branch*' flag—See Section 13.6 [Multiple vendor branches], page 101.). The *release tags* are symbolic names for a particular release, such as 'FSF_0_04'.

Note that `import` does *not* change the directory in which you invoke it. In particular, it does not set up that directory as a CVS working directory; if you want to work with the sources import them first and then check them out into a different directory (see Section 1.3.1 [Getting the source], page 6).

Suppose you have the sources to a program called `wdiff` in a directory 'wdiff-0.04', and are going to make private modifications that you want to be able to use even when new releases are made in the future. You start by importing the source to your repository:

```
$ cd wdiff-0.04
$ cvs import -m "Import of FSF v. 0.04" fsf/wdiff
    FSF_DIST WDIFF_0_04
```

The vendor tag is named 'FSF_DIST' in the above example, and the only release tag assigned is 'WDIFF_0_04'.

13.2 Updating with the import command

When a new release of the source arrives, you import it into the repository with the same import command that you used to set up the repository in the first place. The only difference is that you specify a different release tag this time.

```
$ tar xfz wdiff-0.05.tar.gz
$ cd wdiff-0.05
$ cvs import -m "Import of FSF v. 0.05" fsf/wdiff
    FSF_DIST WDIFF_0_05
```

For files that have not been modified locally, the newly created revision becomes the head revision. If you have made local changes, import will warn you that you must merge the changes into the main trunk, and tell you to use 'checkout -j' to do so.

```
$ cvs checkout -jFSF_DIST:yesterday -jFSF_DIST wdiff
```

The above command will check out the latest revision of 'wdiff', merging the changes made on the vendor branch 'FSF_DIST' since yesterday into the working copy. If any conflicts arise during the merge they should be resolved in the normal way (see Section 10.3 [Conflicts example], page 81). Then, the modified files may be committed.

Using a date, as suggested above, assumes that you do not import more than one release of a product per day. If you do, you can always use something like this instead:

```
$ cvs checkout -jWDIFF_0_04 -jWDIFF_0_05 wdiff
```

In this case, the two above commands are equivalent.

13.3 Reverting to the latest vendor release

You can also revert local changes completely and return to the latest vendor release by changing the 'head' revision back to the vendor branch on all files. For example, if you have a checked-out copy of the sources in '~/work.d/wdiff', and you want to revert to the vendor's version for all the files in that directory, you would type:

```
$ cd ~/work.d/wdiff
$ cvs admin -bWDIFF .
```

You must specify the '-bWDIFF' without any space after the '-b'. See Section A.6.1 [admin options], page 115.

13.4 How to handle binary files with cvs import

Use the '-k' wrapper option to tell import which files are binary. See Section C.2 [Wrappers], page 163.

13.5 How to handle keyword substitution with cvs import

The sources which you are importing may contain keywords (see Chapter 12 [Keyword substitution], page 93). For example, the vendor may use CVS or some other system which uses similar keyword expansion syntax. If you just import the files in the default fashion, then the keyword expansions supplied by the vendor will be replaced by keyword expansions supplied by your own copy of CVS. It may be more convenient to maintain the expansions supplied by the vendor, so that this information can supply information about the sources that you imported from the vendor.

To maintain the keyword expansions supplied by the vendor, supply the '-ko' option to cvs import the first time you import the file. This will turn off keyword expansion for that file entirely, so if you want to be more selective you'll have to think about what you want and use the '-k' option to cvs update or cvs admin as appropriate.

13.6 Multiple vendor branches

All the examples so far assume that there is only one vendor from which you are getting sources. In some situations you might get sources from a variety of places. For example, suppose that you are dealing with a project where many different people and teams are modifying the software. There are a variety of ways to handle this, but in some cases you have a bunch of source trees lying around and what you want to do more than anything else is just to all put them in CVS so that you at least have them in one place.

For handling situations in which there may be more than one vendor, you may specify the '-b' option to cvs import. It takes as an argument the vendor branch to import to. The default is '-b 1.1.1'.

For example, suppose that there are two teams, the red team and the blue team, that are sending you sources. You want to import the red team's efforts to branch 1.1.1 and use the vendor tag RED. You want to import the blue team's efforts to branch 1.1.3 and use the vendor tag BLUE. So the commands you might use are:

```
$ cvs import dir RED RED_1-0
```

```
$ cvs import -b 1.1.3 dir BLUE BLUE_1-5
```

Note that if your vendor tag does not match your '-b' option, CVS will not detect this case! For example,

```
$ cvs import -b 1.1.3 dir RED RED_1-0
```

Be careful; this kind of mismatch is sure to sow confusion or worse. I can't think of a useful purpose for the ability to specify a mismatch here, but if you discover such a use, don't. CVS is likely to make this an error in some future release.

14 How your build system interacts with CVS

As mentioned in the introduction, CVS does not contain software for building your software from source code. This section describes how various aspects of your build system might interact with CVS.

One common question, especially from people who are accustomed to RCS, is how to make their build get an up to date copy of the sources. The answer to this with CVS is two-fold. First of all, since CVS itself can recurse through directories, there is no need to modify your 'Makefile' (or whatever configuration file your build tool uses) to make sure each file is up to date. Instead, just use two commands, first `cvs -q update` and then `make` or whatever the command is to invoke your build tool. Secondly, you do not necessarily *want* to get a copy of a change someone else made until you have finished your own work. One suggested approach is to first update your sources, then implement, build and test the change you were thinking of, and then commit your sources (updating first if necessary). By periodically (in between changes, using the approach just described) updating your entire tree, you ensure that your sources are sufficiently up to date.

One common need is to record which versions of which source files went into a particular build. This kind of functionality is sometimes called *bill of materials* or something similar. The best way to do this with CVS is to use the `tag` command to record which versions went into a given build (see Section 4.4 [Tags], page 44).

Using CVS in the most straightforward manner possible, each developer will have a copy of the entire source tree which is used in a particular build. If the source tree is small, or if developers are geographically dispersed, this is the preferred solution. In fact one approach for larger projects is to break a project down into smaller separately-compiled subsystems, and arrange a way of releasing them internally so that each developer need check out only those subsystems which are they are actively working on.

Another approach is to set up a structure which allows developers to have their own copies of some files, and for other files to access source files from a central location. Many people have come up with some such a system using features such as the symbolic link feature found in many operating systems, or the `VPATH` feature found in many versions of `make`. One build tool which is designed to help with this kind of thing is Odin (see `ftp://ftp.cs.colorado.edu/pub/distribs/odin`).

15 Special Files

In normal circumstances, CVS works only with regular files. Every file in a project is assumed to be persistent; it must be possible to open, read and close them; and so on. CVS also ignores file permissions and ownerships, leaving such issues to be resolved by the developer at installation time. In other words, it is not possible to "check in" a device into a repository; if the device file cannot be opened, CVS will refuse to handle it. Files also lose their ownerships and permissions during repository transactions.

Appendix A Guide to CVS commands

This appendix describes the overall structure of CVS commands, and describes some commands in detail (others are described elsewhere; for a quick reference to CVS commands, see Appendix B [Invoking CVS], page 145).

A.1 Overall structure of CVS commands

The overall format of all CVS commands is:

```
cvs [ cvs_options ]
   cvs_command [ command_options ] [ command_args ]
```

cvs   The name of the CVS program.

cvs_options
                Some options that affect all sub-commands of CVS. These are described below.

cvs_command
                One of several different sub-commands. Some of the commands have aliases that can be used instead; those aliases are noted in the reference manual for that command. There are only two situations where you may omit 'cvs_command': 'cvs -H' elicits a list of available commands, and 'cvs -v' displays version information on CVS itself.

command_options
                Options that are specific for the command.

command_args
                Arguments to the commands.

There is unfortunately some confusion between cvs_options and command_options. '-l', when given as a cvs_option, only affects some of the commands. When it is given as a command_option is has a different meaning, and is accepted by more commands. In other words, do not take the above categorization too seriously. Look at the documentation instead.

A.2 CVS's exit status

CVS can indicate to the calling environment whether it succeeded or failed by setting its *exit status*. The exact way of testing the exit status will vary from one operating system to another. For example in a unix shell script the '$?' variable will be 0 if the last command returned a successful exit status, or greater than 0 if the exit status indicated failure.

If CVS is successful, it returns a successful status; if there is an error, it prints an error message and returns a failure status. The one exception to this is the cvs diff command. It will return a successful status if it found no differences, or a failure status if there were differences or if there was an error. Because this behavior provides no good way to detect errors, in the future it is possible that cvs diff will be changed to behave like the other CVS commands.

A.3 Default options and the ~/.cvsrc file

There are some command_options that are used so often that you might have set up an alias or some other means to make sure you always specify that option. One example (the one that drove the implementation of the '.cvsrc' support, actually) is that many people find the default output of the 'diff' command to be very hard to read, and that either context diffs or unidiffs are much easier to understand.

The '~/.cvsrc' file is a way that you can add default options to cvs_commands within cvs, instead of relying on aliases or other shell scripts.

The format of the '~/.cvsrc' file is simple. The file is searched for a line that begins with the same name as the cvs_command being executed. If a match is found, then the remainder of the line is split up (at whitespace characters) into separate options and added to the command arguments *before* any options from the command line.

If a command has two names (e.g., checkout and co), the official name, not necessarily the one used on the command line, will be used to match against the file. So if this is the contents of the user's '~/.cvsrc' file:

```
log -N
diff -u
update -P
checkout -P
```

the command 'cvs checkout foo' would have the '-P' option added to the arguments, as well as 'cvs co foo'.

With the example file above, the output from 'cvs diff foobar' will be in unidiff format. 'cvs diff -c foobar' will provide context diffs, as usual. Getting "old" format diffs would be slightly more complicated, because diff doesn't have an option to specify use of the "old" format, so you would need 'cvs -f diff foobar'.

In place of the command name you can use cvs to specify global options
(see Section A.4 [Global options], page 109). For example the following
line in '.cvsrc'

        cvs -z6

causes CVS to use compression level 6.

A.4 Global options

The available 'cvs_options' (that are given to the left of 'cvs_command')
are:

--allow-root=*rootdir*

Specify legal CVSROOT directory. See Section 2.9.3.1 [Pass-
word authentication server], page 29.

-a   Authenticate all communication between the client and the
                server. Only has an effect on the CVS client. As of this
                writing, this is only implemented when using a GSSAPI con-
                nection (see Section 2.9.4 [GSSAPI authenticated], page 34).
                Authentication prevents certain sorts of attacks involving hi-
                jacking the active TCP connection. Enabling authentication
                does not enable encryption.

-b *bindir*   In CVS 1.9.18 and older, this specified that RCS programs are
                in the *bindir* directory. Current versions of CVS do not run
                RCS programs; for compatibility this option is accepted, but
                it does nothing.

-T *tempdir*   Use *tempdir* as the directory where temporary files are lo-
                cated. Overrides the setting of the $TMPDIR environment
                variable and any precompiled directory. This parameter
                should be specified as an absolute pathname.

-d *cvs_root_directory*

Use *cvs_root_directory* as the root directory pathname of the
repository. Overrides the setting of the $CVSROOT environ-
ment variable. See Chapter 2 [Repository], page 11.

-e *editor*   Use *editor* to enter revision log information. Overrides the
                setting of the $CVSEDITOR and $EDITOR environment vari-
                ables. For more information, see Section 1.3.2 [Committing
                your changes], page 7.

-f   Do not read the '~/.cvsrc' file. This option is most often
                used because of the non-orthogonality of the CVS option set.
                For example, the 'cvs log' option '-N' (turn off display of

tag names) does not have a corresponding option to turn the display on. So if you have '-N' in the '˜/.cvsrc' entry for 'log', you may need to use '-f' to show the tag names.

-H

--help   Display usage information about the specified 'cvs_command' (but do not actually execute the command). If you don't specify a command name, 'cvs -H' displays overall help for CVS, including a list of other help options.

-l   Do not log the 'cvs_command' in the command history (but execute it anyway). See Section A.11 [history], page 129, for information on command history.

-n   Do not change any files. Attempt to execute the 'cvs_command', but only to issue reports; do not remove, update, or merge any existing files, or create any new files.

                Note that CVS will not necessarily produce exactly the same output as without '-n'. In some cases the output will be the same, but in other cases CVS will skip some of the processing that would have been required to produce the exact same output.

-Q   Cause the command to be really quiet; the command will only generate output for serious problems.

-q   Cause the command to be somewhat quiet; informational messages, such as reports of recursion through subdirectories, are suppressed.

-r   Make new working files read-only. Same effect as if the $CVSREAD environment variable is set (see Appendix D [Environment variables], page 177). The default is to make working files writable, unless watches are on (see Section 10.6 [Watches], page 85).

-s variable=value
                Set a user variable (see Section C.12 [Variables], page 173).

-t   Trace program execution; display messages showing the steps of CVS activity. Particularly useful with '-n' to explore the potential impact of an unfamiliar command.

-v

--version   Display version and copyright information for CVS.

-w   Make new working files read-write. Overrides the setting of the $CVSREAD environment variable. Files are created read-write by default, unless $CVSREAD is set or '-r' is given.

-x   Encrypt all communication between the client and the server. Only has an effect on the CVS client. As of this writing, this is only implemented when using a GSSAPI connection (see Section 2.9.4 [GSSAPI authenticated], page 34) or a Kerberos connection (see Section 2.9.5 [Kerberos authenticated], page 34). Enabling encryption implies that message traffic is also authenticated. Encryption support is not available by default; it must be enabled using a special configure option, '--enable-encryption', when you build CVS.

-z *gzip-level*

Set the compression level. Valid levels are 1 (high speed, low compression) to 9 (low speed, high compression), or 0 to disable compression (the default). Only has an effect on the CVS client.

A.5 Common command options

This section describes the 'command_options' that are available across several CVS commands. These options are always given to the right of 'cvs_command'. Not all commands support all of these options; each option is only supported for commands where it makes sense. However, when a command has one of these options you can almost always count on the same behavior of the option as in other commands. (Other command options, which are listed with the individual commands, may have different behavior from one CVS command to the other).

Warning: the 'history' command is an exception; it supports many options that conflict even with these standard options.

-D *date_spec*

Use the most recent revision no later than *date_spec*. *date_spec* is a single argument, a date description specifying a date in the past.

The specification is *sticky* when you use it to make a private copy of a source file; that is, when you get a working file using '-D', CVS records the date you specified, so that further updates in the same directory will use the same date (for more information on sticky tags/dates, see Section 4.9 [Sticky tags], page 50).

'-D' is available with the checkout, diff, export, history, rdiff, rtag, and update commands. (The history command uses this option in a slightly different way; see Section A.11.1 [history options], page 130).

A wide variety of date formats are supported by CVS. The most standard ones are ISO8601 (from the International Standards Organization) and the Internet e-mail standard (specified in RFC822 as amended by RFC1123).

ISO8601 dates have many variants but a few examples are:

```
1972-09-24
1972-09-24 20:05
```

There are a lot more ISO8601 date formats, and CVS accepts many of them, but you probably don't want to hear the *whole* long story :-).

In addition to the dates allowed in Internet e-mail itself, CVS also allows some of the fields to be omitted. For example:

```
24 Sep 1972 20:05
24 Sep
```

The date is interpreted as being in the local timezone, unless a specific timezone is specified.

These two date formats are preferred. However, CVS currently accepts a wide variety of other date formats. They are intentionally not documented here in any detail, and future versions of CVS might not accept all of them.

One such format is *month/day/year*. This may confuse people who are accustomed to having the month and day in the other order; '1/4/96' is January 4, not April 1.

Remember to quote the argument to the '-D' flag so that your shell doesn't interpret spaces as argument separators. A command using the '-D' flag can look like this:

```
$ cvs diff -D "1 hour ago" cvs.texinfo
```

-f   When you specify a particular date or tag to CVS commands, they normally ignore files that do not contain the tag (or did not exist prior to the date) that you specified. Use the '-f' option if you want files retrieved even when there is no match for the tag or date. (The most recent revision of the file will be used).

Note that even with '-f', a tag that you specify must exist (that is, in some file, not necessary in every file). This is so that CVS will continue to give an error if you mistype a tag name.

'-f' is available with these commands: `annotate`, `checkout`, `export`, `rdiff`, `rtag`, and `update`.

Warning: The `commit` and `remove` commands also have a '-f' option, but it has a different behavior for those commands. See Section A.8.1 [commit options], page 124, and Section 7.2 [Removing files], page 66.

-k *kflag*   Alter the default processing of keywords. See Chapter 12 [Keyword substitution], page 93, for the meaning of *kflag*. Your *kflag* specification is *sticky* when you use it to create a private copy of a source file; that is, when you use this option with the `checkout` or `update` commands, CVS associates your selected *kflag* with the file, and continues to use it with future update commands on the same file until you specify otherwise.

The '-k' option is available with the `add`, `checkout`, `diff`, `import` and `update` commands.

-l   Local; run only in current working directory, rather than recursing through subdirectories.

Warning: this is not the same as the overall 'cvs -l' option, which you can specify to the left of a cvs command!

Available with the following commands: `annotate`, `checkout`, `commit`, `diff`, `edit`, `editors`, `export`, `log`, `rdiff`, `remove`, `rtag`, `status`, `tag`, `unedit`, `update`, `watch`, and `watchers`.

-m *message*   Use *message* as log information, instead of invoking an editor.

Available with the following commands: `add`, `commit` and `import`.

-n   Do not run any checkout/commit/tag program. (A program can be specified to run on each of these activities, in the modules database (see Section C.1 [modules], page 159); this option bypasses it).

Warning: this is not the same as the overall 'cvs -n' option, which you can specify to the left of a cvs command!

Available with the `checkout`, `commit`, `export`, and `rtag` commands.

-P   Prune empty directories. See Section 7.3 [Removing directories], page 68.

-p   Pipe the files retrieved from the repository to standard output, rather than writing them in the current directory. Available with the `checkout` and `update` commands.

-R   Process directories recursively. This is on by default.

            Available with the following commands: `annotate`, `checkout`, `commit`, `diff`, `edit`, `editors`, `export`, `rdiff`, `remove`, `rtag`, `status`, `tag`, `unedit`, `update`, `watch`, and `watchers`.

-r *tag*   Use the revision specified by the *tag* argument instead of the default *head* revision. As well as arbitrary tags defined with the `tag` or `rtag` command, two special tags are always available: 'HEAD' refers to the most recent version available in the repository, and 'BASE' refers to the revision you last checked out into the current working directory.

            The tag specification is sticky when you use this with `checkout` or `update` to make your own copy of a file: CVS remembers the tag and continues to use it on future update commands, until you specify otherwise (for more information on sticky tags/dates, see Section 4.9 [Sticky tags], page 50).

            The tag can be either a symbolic or numeric tag, as described in Section 4.4 [Tags], page 44, or the name of a branch, as described in Chapter 5 [Branching and merging], page 53.

            Specifying the '-q' global option along with the '-r' command option is often useful, to suppress the warning messages when the RCS file does not contain the specified tag.

            Warning: this is not the same as the overall 'cvs -r' option, which you can specify to the left of a CVS command!

            '-r' is available with the `checkout`, `commit`, `diff`, `history`, `export`, `rdiff`, `rtag`, and `update` commands.

-W   Specify file names that should be filtered. You can use this option repeatedly. The spec can be a file name pattern of the same type that you can specify in the '.cvswrappers' file. Available with the following commands: `import`, and `update`.

A.6 admin—Administration

- Requires: repository, working directory.
- Changes: repository.
- Synonym: rcs

This is the CVS interface to assorted administrative facilities. Some of
them have questionable usefulness for CVS but exist for historical purposes.
Some of the questionable options are likely to disappear in the future. This
command *does* work recursively, so extreme care should be used.

On unix, if there is a group named cvsadmin, only members of that group
can run cvs admin (except for the cvs admin -k command, which can be
run by anybody). This group should exist on the server, or any system
running the non-client/server CVS. To disallow cvs admin for all users,
create a group with no users in it. On NT, the cvsadmin feature does not
exist and all users can run cvs admin.

A.6.1 admin options

Some of these options have questionable usefulness for CVS but exist for
historical purposes. Some even make it impossible to use CVS until you
undo the effect!

-A*oldfile*   Might not work together with CVS. Append the access list
              of *oldfile* to the access list of the RCS file.

-a*logins*   Might not work together with CVS. Append the login names
              appearing in the comma-separated list *logins* to the access
              list of the RCS file.

-b[*rev*]   Set the default branch to *rev*. In CVS, you normally do not
              manipulate default branches; sticky tags (see Section 4.9
              [Sticky tags], page 50) are a better way to decide which
              branch you want to work on. There is one reason to run
              cvs admin -b: to revert to the vendor's version when using
              vendor branches (see Section 13.3 [Reverting local changes],
              page 100). There can be no space between '-b' and its ar-
              gument.

-c*string*   Sets the comment leader to *string*. The comment leader is
              not used by current versions of CVS or RCS 5.7. Therefore,
              you can almost surely not worry about it. See Chapter 12
              [Keyword substitution], page 93.

-e[*logins*]   Might not work together with CVS. Erase the login names
              appearing in the comma-separated list *logins* from the ac-
              cess list of the RCS file. If *logins* is omitted, erase the entire
              access list. There can be no space between '-e' and its ar-
              gument.

-I   Run interactively, even if the standard input is not a termi-
              nal. This option does not work with the client/server CVS
              and is likely to disappear in a future release of CVS.

-i   Useless with CVS. This creates and initializes a new RCS file,
                without depositing a revision. With CVS, add files with the
                cvs add command (see Section 7.1 [Adding files], page 65).

-k*subst*   Set the default keyword substitution to *subst*. See Chap-
                ter 12 [Keyword substitution], page 93. Giving an explicit
                '-k' option to **cvs update**, **cvs export**, or **cvs checkout**
                overrides this default.

-l[*rev*]   Lock the revision with number *rev*. If a branch is given, lock
                the latest revision on that branch. If *rev* is omitted, lock the
                latest revision on the default branch. There can be no space
                between '-l' and its argument.

                This can be used in conjunction with the 'rcslock.pl' script
                in the 'contrib' directory of the CVS source distribution
                to provide reserved checkouts (where only one user can be
                editing a given file at a time). See the comments in that
                file for details (and see the 'README' file in that directory
                for disclaimers about the unsupported nature of contrib).
                According to comments in that file, locking must set to strict
                (which is the default).

-L   Set locking to strict. Strict locking means that the owner
                of an RCS file is not exempt from locking for checkin. For
                use with CVS, strict locking must be set; see the discussion
                under the '-l' option above.

-m*rev*:*msg*   Replace the log message of revision *rev* with *msg*.

-N*name*[:[*rev*]]
                Act like '-n', except override any previous assignment of
                name. For use with magic branches, see Section 5.5 [Magic
                branch numbers], page 56.

-n*name*[:[*rev*]]
                Associate the symbolic name *name* with the branch or re-
                vision *rev*. It is normally better to use 'cvs tag' or 'cvs
                rtag' instead. Delete the symbolic name if both ':' and *rev*
                are omitted; otherwise, print an error message if *name* is al-
                ready associated with another number. If *rev* is symbolic, it
                is expanded before association. A *rev* consisting of a branch
                number followed by a '.' stands for the current latest revi-
                sion in the branch. A ':' with an empty *rev* stands for the
                current latest revision on the default branch, normally the
                trunk. For example, 'cvs admin -n*name*:' associates *name*
                with the current latest revision of all the RCS files; this

contrasts with 'cvs admin -nname:$' which associates *name* with the revision numbers extracted from keyword strings in the corresponding working files.

-orange   Deletes (*outdates*) the revisions given by *range*.

Note that this command can be quite dangerous unless you know *exactly* what you are doing (for example see the warnings below about how the *rev1:rev2* syntax is confusing).

If you are short on disc this option might help you. But think twice before using it—there is no way short of restoring the latest backup to undo this command! If you delete different revisions than you planned, either due to carelessness or (heaven forbid) a CVS bug, there is no opportunity to correct the error before the revisions are deleted. It probably would be a good idea to experiment on a copy of the repository first.

Specify *range* in one of the following ways:

rev1::rev2   Collapse all revisions between rev1 and rev2, so that CVS only stores the differences associated with going from rev1 to rev2, not intermediate steps. For example, after '-o 1.3::1.5' one can retrieve revision 1.3, revision 1.5, or the differences to get from 1.3 to 1.5, but not the revision 1.4, or the differences between 1.3 and 1.4. Other examples: '-o 1.3::1.4' and '-o 1.3::1.3' have no effect, because there are no intermediate revisions to remove.

::*rev*   Collapse revisions between the beginning of the branch containing *rev* and *rev* itself. The branchpoint and *rev* are left intact. For example, '-o ::1.3.2.6' deletes revision 1.3.2.1, revision 1.3.2.5, and everything in between, but leaves 1.3 and 1.3.2.6 intact.

rev::   Collapse revisions between *rev* and the end of the branch containing *rev*. Revision *rev* is left intact but the head revision is deleted.

rev   Delete the revision *rev*. For example, '-o 1.3' is equivalent to '-o 1.2::1.4'.

rev1:rev2   Delete the revisions from *rev1* to *rev2*, inclusive, on the same branch. One will not be able to retrieve *rev1* or *rev2* or any of the revisions in between. For example, the command 'cvs admin -oR_1_01:R_1_02 .' is rarely useful. It means to delete revisions up to, and including, the tag R_1_02. But beware! If there are files that have not changed between R_1_02 and R_1_03 the file will have *the same* numerical revision number assigned to the tags R_1_02 and R_1_03. So not only will it be impossible to retrieve R_1_02; R_1_03 will also have to be restored from the tapes! In most cases you want to specify *rev1::rev2* instead.

:rev   Delete revisions from the beginning of the branch containing *rev* up to and including *rev*.

rev: Delete revisions from revision *rev*, including *rev* itself, to the end of the branch containing *rev*.

None of the revisions to be deleted may have branches or locks.

If any of the revisions to be deleted have symbolic names, and one specifies one of the ':: ' syntaxes, then CVS will give an error and not delete any revisions. If you really want to delete both the symbolic names and the revisions, first delete the symbolic names with cvs **tag** -d, then run cvs admin -o. If one specifies the non-':: ' syntaxes, then CVS will delete the revisions but leave the symbolic names pointing to nonexistent revisions. This behavior is preserved for compatibility with previous versions of CVS, but because it isn't very useful, in the future it may change to be like the ':: ' case.

Due to the way CVS handles branches *rev* cannot be specified symbolically if it is a branch. See Section 5.5 [Magic branch numbers], page 56, for an explanation.

Make sure that no-one has checked out a copy of the revision you outdate. Strange things will happen if he starts to edit it and tries to check it back in. For this reason, this option is not a good way to take back a bogus commit; commit a new revision undoing the bogus change instead (see Section 5.8 [Merging two revisions], page 59).

-q   Run quietly; do not print diagnostics.

-s*state*[:*rev*]

    Useful with CVS. Set the state attribute of the revision *rev* to *state*. If *rev* is a branch number, assume the latest revision on that branch. If *rev* is omitted, assume the latest revision on the default branch. Any identifier is acceptable for *state*. A useful set of states is 'Exp' (for experimental), 'Stab' (for stable), and 'Rel' (for released). By default, the state of a new revision is set to 'Exp' when it is created. The state is visible in the output from *cvs log* (see Section A.13 [log], page 134), and in the 'Log' and '$State$' keywords (see Chapter 12 [Keyword substitution], page 93). Note that CVS uses the **dead** state for its own purposes; to take a file to or from the **dead** state use commands like **cvs remove** and **cvs add**, not **cvs admin -s**.

-t [*file*]   Useful with CVS. Write descriptive text from the contents of the named *file* into the RCS file, deleting the existing text. The *file* pathname may not begin with '-'. The descriptive text can be seen in the output from 'cvs log' (see Section A.13 [log], page 134). There can be no space between '-t' and its argument.

If *file* is omitted, obtain the text from standard input, terminated by end-of-file or by a line containing '.' by itself. Prompt for the text if interaction is possible; see '-I'.

-t-*string*   Similar to '-t*file*'. Write descriptive text from the *string* into the RCS file, deleting the existing text. There can be no space between '-t' and its argument.

-U   Set locking to non-strict. Non-strict locking means that the owner of a file need not lock a revision for checkin. For use with CVS, strict locking must be set; see the discussion under the '-l' option above.

-u[*rev*]   See the option '-l' above, for a discussion of using this option with CVS. Unlock the revision with number *rev*. If a branch is given, unlock the latest revision on that branch. If *rev* is omitted, remove the latest lock held by the caller. Normally, only the locker of a revision may unlock it. Somebody else unlocking a revision breaks the lock. This causes a mail message to be sent to the original locker. The message contains a commentary solicited from the breaker. The commentary is terminated by end-of-file or by a line containing . by itself. There can be no space between '-u' and its argument.

-V*n*   In previous versions of CVS, this option meant to write an RCS file which would be acceptable to RCS version *n*, but it is now obsolete and specifying it will produce an error.

-xsuffixes   In previous versions of CVS, this was documented as a way
             of specifying the names of the RCS files. However, CVS has
             always required that the RCS files used by CVS end in ',v',
             so this option has never done anything useful.

A.7 checkout—Check out sources for editing

- Synopsis: checkout [options] modules...
- Requires: repository.
- Changes: working directory.
- Synonyms: co, get

Create or update a working directory containing copies of the source files
specified by *modules*. You must execute checkout before using most of
the other CVS commands, since most of them operate on your working
directory.

The *modules* are either symbolic names for some collection of source directories and files, or paths to directories or files in the repository. The
symbolic names are defined in the 'modules' file. See Section C.1 [mod-
ules], page 159.

Depending on the modules you specify, checkout may recursively create
directories and populate them with the appropriate source files.   You
can then edit these source files at any time (regardless of whether other
software developers are editing their own copies of the sources); update
them to include new changes applied by others to the source repository;
or commit your work as a permanent change to the source repository.

Note that checkout is used to create directories. The top-level directory
created is always added to the directory where checkout is invoked, and
usually has the same name as the specified module. In the case of a
module alias, the created sub-directory may have a different name, but
you can be sure that it will be a sub-directory, and that checkout will
show the relative path leading to each file as it is extracted into your
private work area (unless you specify the '-Q' global option).

The files created by checkout are created read-write, unless the '-r' option to CVS (see Section A.4 [Global options], page 109) is specified, the
CVSREAD environment variable is specified (see Appendix D [Environment
variables], page 177), or a watch is in effect for that file (see Section 10.6
[Watches], page 85).

Note that running checkout on a directory that was already built by a
prior checkout is also permitted. This is similar to specifying the '-d'
option to the update command in the sense that new directories that have
been created in the repository will appear in your work area. However,

checkout takes a module name whereas update takes a directory name. Also to use checkout this way it must be run from the top level directory (where you originally ran checkout from), so before you run checkout to update an existing directory, don't forget to change your directory to the top level directory.

For the output produced by the checkout command see Section A.16.2 [update output], page 142.

A.7.1 checkout options

These standard options are supported by checkout (see Section A.5 [Common options], page 111, for a complete description of them):

-D *date*   Use the most recent revision no later than *date*. This option is sticky, and implies '-P'. See Section 4.9 [Sticky tags], page 50, for more information on sticky tags/dates.

-f   Only useful with the '-D *date*' or '-r *tag*' flags. If no matching revision is found, retrieve the most recent revision (instead of ignoring the file).

-k *kflag*   Process keywords according to *kflag*. See Chapter 12 [Keyword substitution], page 93. This option is sticky; future updates of this file in this working directory will use the same *kflag*. The status command can be viewed to see the sticky options. See Appendix B [Invoking CVS], page 145, for more information on the status command.

-l   Local; run only in current working directory.

-n   Do not run any checkout program (as specified with the '-o' option in the modules file; see Section C.1 [modules], page 159).

-P   Prune empty directories. See Section 7.5 [Moving directories], page 70.

-p   Pipe files to the standard output.

-R   Checkout directories recursively. This option is on by default.

-r *tag*   Use revision *tag*. This option is sticky, and implies '-P'. See Section 4.9 [Sticky tags], page 50, for more information on sticky tags/dates.

In addition to those, you can use these special command options with checkout:

-A   Reset any sticky tags, dates, or '-k' options. See Section 4.9 [Sticky tags], page 50, for more information on sticky tags/dates.

-c   Copy the module file, sorted, to the standard output, instead of creating or modifying any files or directories in your working directory.

-d *dir*   Create a directory called *dir* for the working files, instead of using the module name. In general, using this flag is equivalent to using 'mkdir *dir*; cd *dir*' followed by the checkout command without the '-d' flag.

              There is an important exception, however. It is very convenient when checking out a single item to have the output appear in a directory that doesn't contain empty intermediate directories. In this case *only*, CVS tries to "shorten" pathnames to avoid those empty directories.

              For example, given a module 'foo' that contains the file 'bar.c', the command 'cvs co -d dir foo' will create directory 'dir' and place 'bar.c' inside. Similarly, given a module 'bar' which has subdirectory 'baz' wherein there is a file 'quux.c', the command 'cvs -d dir co bar/baz' will create directory 'dir' and place 'quux.c' inside.

              Using the '-N' flag will defeat this behavior. Given the same module definitions above, 'cvs co -N -d dir foo' will create directories 'dir/foo' and place 'bar.c' inside, while 'cvs co -N -d dir bar/baz' will create directories 'dir/bar/baz' and place 'quux.c' inside.

-j *tag*   With two '-j' options, merge changes from the revision specified with the first '-j' option to the revision specified with the second 'j' option, into the working directory.

              With one '-j' option, merge changes from the ancestor revision to the revision specified with the '-j' option, into the working directory. The ancestor revision is the common ancestor of the revision which the working directory is based on, and the revision specified in the '-j' option.

              In addition, each -j option can contain an optional date specification which, when used with branches, can limit the chosen revision to one within a specific date. An optional date is specified by adding a colon (:) to the tag: '-j*Symbolic_Tag*:*Date_Specifier*'.

              See Chapter 5 [Branching and merging], page 53.

-N   Only useful together with '-d *dir*'. With this option, CVS
                  will not "shorten" module paths in your working directory
                  when you check out a single module. See the '-d' flag for
                  examples and a discussion.

-s   Like '-c', but include the status of all modules, and sort it
                  by the status string. See Section C.1 [modules], page 159,
                  for info about the '-s' option that is used inside the modules
                  file to set the module status.

A.7.2 checkout examples

Get a copy of the module 'tc':

    $ cvs checkout tc

Get a copy of the module 'tc' as it looked one day ago:

    $ cvs checkout -D yesterday tc

A.8 commit—Check files into the repository

- Synopsis: commit [-lnRf] [-m 'log_message' | -F file] [-r revision]
  [files. . .]
- Requires: working directory, repository.
- Changes: repository.
- Synonym: ci

Use commit when you want to incorporate changes from your working
source files into the source repository.

If you don't specify particular files to commit, all of the files in your
working current directory are examined. commit is careful to change in
the repository only those files that you have really changed. By default
(or if you explicitly specify the '-R' option), files in subdirectories are
also examined and committed if they have changed; you can use the '-l'
option to limit commit to the current directory only.

commit verifies that the selected files are up to date with the current
revisions in the source repository; it will notify you, and exit without
committing, if any of the specified files must be made current first with
update (see Section A.16 [update], page 140). commit does not call the
update command for you, but rather leaves that for you to do when the
time is right.

When all is well, an editor is invoked to allow you to enter a log message
that will be written to one or more logging programs (see Section C.1
[modules], page 159, and see Section C.7 [loginfo], page 169) and placed
in the RCS file inside the repository. This log message can be retrieved

with the `log` command; see Section A.13 [log], page 134. You can specify
the log message on the command line with the '-m *message*' option, and
thus avoid the editor invocation, or use the '-F *file*' option to specify that
the argument file contains the log message.

A.8.1 commit options

These standard options are supported by `commit` (see Section A.5 [Common options], page 111, for a complete description of them):

-l   Local; run only in current working directory.

-n   Do not run any module program.

-R   Commit directories recursively. This is on by default.

-r *revision* Commit to *revision*. *revision* must be either a branch, or
            a revision on the main trunk that is higher than any exist-
            ing revision number (see Section 4.3 [Assigning revisions],
            page 43). You cannot commit to a specific revision on a
            branch.

`commit` also supports these options:

-F *file*   Read the log message from *file*, instead of invoking an editor.

-f   Note that this is not the standard behavior of the '-f' option
            as defined in Section A.5 [Common options], page 111.

            Force CVS to commit a new revision even if you haven't made
            any changes to the file. If the current revision of *file* is 1.7,
            then the following two commands are equivalent:

                $ cvs commit -f *file*
                $ cvs commit -r 1.8 *file*

            The '-f' option disables recursion (i.e., it implies '-l'). To
            force CVS to commit a new revision for all files in all subdi-
            rectories, you must use '-f -R'.

-m *message* Use *message* as the log message, instead of invoking an edi-
            tor.

A.8.2 commit examples

A.8.2.1 Committing to a branch

You can commit to a branch revision (one that has an even number of dots) with the '-r' option. To create a branch revision, use the '-b' option of the rtag or tag commands (see Chapter 5 [Branching and merging], page 53). Then, either checkout or update can be used to base your sources on the newly created branch. From that point on, all commit changes made within these working sources will be automatically added to a branch revision, thereby not disturbing main-line development in any way. For example, if you had to create a patch to the 1.2 version of the product, even though the 2.0 version is already under development, you might do:

```
$ cvs rtag -b -r FCS1_2 FCS1_2_Patch product_module
$ cvs checkout -r FCS1_2_Patch product_module
$ cd product_module
[[ hack away ]]
$ cvs commit
```

This works automatically since the '-r' option is sticky.

A.8.2.2 Creating the branch after editing

Say you have been working on some extremely experimental software, based on whatever revision you happened to checkout last week. If others in your group would like to work on this software with you, but without disturbing main-line development, you could commit your change to a new branch. Others can then checkout your experimental stuff and utilize the full benefit of CVS conflict resolution. The scenario might look like:

```
[[ hacked sources are present ]]
$ cvs tag -b EXPR1
$ cvs update -r EXPR1
$ cvs commit
```

The update command will make the '-r EXPR1' option sticky on all files. Note that your changes to the files will never be removed by the update command. The commit will automatically commit to the correct branch, because the '-r' is sticky. You could also do like this:

```
[[ hacked sources are present ]]
$ cvs tag -b EXPR1
$ cvs commit -r EXPR1
```

but then, only those files that were changed by you will have the '-r
EXPR1' sticky flag. If you hack away, and commit without specifying the
'-r EXPR1' flag, some files may accidentally end up on the main trunk.

To work with you on the experimental change, others would simply do

```
$ cvs checkout -r EXPR1 whatever_module
```

A.9 diff—Show differences between revisions

- Synopsis: diff [-lR] [format_options] [[-r rev1 | -D date1] [-r rev2 | -D date2]] [files. . .]
- Requires: working directory, repository.
- Changes: nothing.

The diff command is used to compare different revisions of files. The
default action is to compare your working files with the revisions they
were based on, and report any differences that are found.

If any file names are given, only those files are compared. If any directories
are given, all files under them will be compared.

The exit status for diff is different than for other CVS commands; for
details Section A.2 [Exit status], page 107.

A.9.1 diff options

These standard options are supported by diff (see Section A.5 [Common
options], page 111, for a complete description of them):

-D date   Use the most recent revision no later than date. See '-r' for
             how this affects the comparison.

-k kflag   Process keywords according to kflag. See Chapter 12 [Key-
             word substitution], page 93.

-l   Local; run only in current working directory.

-R   Examine directories recursively. This option is on by default.

-r tag   Compare with revision tag. Zero, one or two '-r' options
             can be present. With no '-r' option, the working file will be
             compared with the revision it was based on. With one '-r',
             that revision will be compared to your current working file.
             With two '-r' options those two revisions will be compared
             (and your working file will not affect the outcome in any
             way).

             One or both '-r' options can be replaced by a '-D date' op-
             tion, described above.

The following options specify the format of the output. They have the same meaning as in GNU diff.

```
-0 -1 -2 -3 -4 -5 -6 -7 -8 -9
--binary
--brief
--changed-group-format=arg
-c
  -C nlines
  --context[=lines]
-e --ed
-t --expand-tabs
-f --forward-ed
--horizon-lines=arg
--ifdef=arg
-w --ignore-all-space
-B --ignore-blank-lines
-i --ignore-case
-I regexp
   --ignore-matching-lines=regexp
-h
-b --ignore-space-change
-T --initial-tab
-L label
  --label=label
--left-column
-d --minimal
-N --new-file
--new-line-format=arg
--old-line-format=arg
--paginate
-n --rcs
-s --report-identical-files
-p
--show-c-function
-y --side-by-side
-F regexp
--show-function-line=regexp
-H --speed-large-files
--suppress-common-lines
-a --text
--unchanged-group-format=arg
```

```
-u
  -U nlines
  --unified[=lines]
-V arg
-W columns
  --width=columns
```

A.9.2 diff examples

The following line produces a Unidiff ('-u' flag) between revision 1.14 and
1.19 of 'backend.c'. Due to the '-kk' flag no keywords are substituted,
so differences that only depend on keyword substitution are ignored.

```
$ cvs diff -kk -u -r 1.14 -r 1.19 backend.c
```

Suppose the experimental branch EXPR1 was based on a set of files tagged
RELEASE_1_0. To see what has happened on that branch, the following
can be used:

```
$ cvs diff -r RELEASE_1_0 -r EXPR1
```

A command like this can be used to produce a context diff between two
releases:

```
$ cvs diff -c -r RELEASE_1_0 -r RELEASE_1_1 > diffs
```

If you are maintaining ChangeLogs, a command like the following just
before you commit your changes may help you write the ChangeLog entry.
All local modifications that have not yet been committed will be printed.

```
$ cvs diff -u | less
```

A.10 export—Export sources from CVS, similar to checkout

- Synopsis: export [-flNnR] [-r rev|-D date] [-k subst] [-d dir] module...
- Requires: repository.
- Changes: current directory.

This command is a variant of checkout; use it when you want a copy
of the source for module without the CVS administrative directories. For
example, you might use export to prepare source for shipment off-site.
This command requires that you specify a date or tag (with '-D' or '-r'),
so that you can count on reproducing the source you ship to others (and
thus it always prunes empty directories).

One often would like to use '-kv' with cvs export. This causes any
keywords to be expanded such that an import done at some other site
will not lose the keyword revision information. But be aware that doesn't

handle an export containing binary files correctly. Also be aware that after having used '-kv', one can no longer use the ident command (which is part of the RCS suite—see ident(1)) which looks for keyword strings. If you want to be able to use ident you must not use '-kv'.

A.10.1 export options

These standard options are supported by export (see Section A.5 [Common options], page 111, for a complete description of them):

-D *date*   Use the most recent revision no later than *date*.

-f   If no matching revision is found, retrieve the most recent revision (instead of ignoring the file).

-l   Local; run only in current working directory.

-n   Do not run any checkout program.

-R   Export directories recursively. This is on by default.

-r *tag*   Use revision *tag*.

In addition, these options (that are common to checkout and export) are also supported:

-d *dir*   Create a directory called *dir* for the working files, instead of using the module name. See Section A.7.1 [checkout options], page 121, for complete details on how CVS handles this flag.

-k *subst*   Set keyword expansion mode (see Section 12.4 [Substitution modes], page 95).

-N   Only useful together with '-d *dir*'. See Section A.7.1 [checkout options], page 121, for complete details on how CVS handles this flag.

A.11 history—Show status of files and users

- Synopsis: history [-report] [-flags] [-options args] [files...]
- Requires: the file '$CVSROOT/CVSROOT/history'
- Changes: nothing.

CVS can keep a history file that tracks each use of the checkout, commit, rtag, update, and release commands. You can use history to display this information in various formats.

Logging must be enabled by creating the file '$CVSROOT/CVSROOT/history'.

Warning: history uses '-f', '-l', '-n', and '-p' in ways that conflict with the normal use inside CVS (see Section A.5 [Common options], page 111).

A.11.1 history options

Several options (shown above as '-report') control what kind of report
is generated:

-c   Report on each time commit was used (i.e., each time the
                repository was modified).

-e   Everything (all record types). Equivalent to specifying '-x'
                with all record types. Of course, '-e' will also include record
                types which are added in a future version of CVS; if you are
                writing a script which can only handle certain record types,
                you'll want to specify '-x'.

-m *module*   Report on a particular module. (You can meaningfully use
                '-m' more than once on the command line.)

-o   Report on checked-out modules. This is the default report
                type.

-T   Report on all tags.

-x *type*   Extract a particular set of record types *type* from the CVS
                history. The types are indicated by single letters, which you
                may specify in combination.

                Certain commands have a single record type:

                F   release

                O   checkout

                E   export

                T   rtag

                One of four record types may result from an update:

                C   A merge was necessary but collisions were de-
                             tected (requiring manual merging).

                G   A merge was necessary and it succeeded.

                U   A working file was copied from the repository.

                W   The working copy of a file was deleted during
                             update (because it was gone from the reposi-
                             tory).

                One of three record types results from commit:

                A   A file was added for the first time.

                M   A file was modified.

R   A file was removed.

The options shown as '-flags' constrain or expand the report without requiring option arguments:

-a   Show data for all users (the default is to show data only for the user executing history).

-l   Show last modification only.

-w   Show only the records for modifications done from the same working directory where history is executing.

The options shown as '-options args' constrain the report based on an argument:

-b str   Show data back to a record containing the string str in either the module name, the file name, or the repository path.

-D date   Show data since date. This is slightly different from the normal use of '-D date', which selects the newest revision older than date.

-f file   Show data for a particular file (you can specify several '-f' options on the same command line). This is equivalent to specifying the file on the command line.

-n module   Show data for a particular module (you can specify several '-n' options on the same command line).

-p repository
                Show data for a particular source repository (you can specify several '-p' options on the same command line).

-r rev   Show records referring to revisions since the revision or tag named rev appears in individual RCS files. Each RCS file is searched for the revision or tag.

-t tag   Show records since tag tag was last added to the history file. This differs from the '-r' flag above in that it reads only the history file, not the RCS files, and is much faster.

-u name   Show records for user name.

-z timezone
                Show times in the selected records using the specified time zone instead of UTC.

A.12 import—Import sources into CVS, using vendor branches

- Synopsis: import [-options] repository vendortag releasetag...

- Requires: Repository, source distribution directory.

- Changes: repository.

Use import to incorporate an entire source distribution from an outside source (e.g., a source vendor) into your source repository directory. You can use this command both for initial creation of a repository, and for wholesale updates to the module from the outside source. See Chapter 13 [Tracking sources], page 99, for a discussion on this subject.

The *repository* argument gives a directory name (or a path to a directory) under the CVS root directory for repositories; if the directory did not exist, import creates it.

When you use import for updates to source that has been modified in your source repository (since a prior import), it will notify you of any files that conflict in the two branches of development; use 'checkout -j' to reconcile the differences, as import instructs you to do.

If CVS decides a file should be ignored (see Section C.9 [cvsignore], page 171), it does not import it and prints 'I ' followed by the filename (see Section A.12.2 [import output], page 133, for a complete description of the output).

If the file '$CVSROOT/CVSROOT/cvswrappers' exists, any file whose names match the specifications in that file will be treated as packages and the appropriate filtering will be performed on the file/directory before being imported. See Section C.2 [Wrappers], page 163.

The outside source is saved in a first-level branch, by default 1.1.1. Updates are leaves of this branch; for example, files from the first imported collection of source will be revision 1.1.1.1, then files from the first imported update will be revision 1.1.1.2, and so on.

At least three arguments are required. *repository* is needed to identify the collection of source. *vendortag* is a tag for the entire branch (e.g., for 1.1.1). You must also specify at least one *releasetag* to identify the files at the leaves created each time you execute import.

Note that import does *not* change the directory in which you invoke it. In particular, it does not set up that directory as a CVS working directory; if you want to work with the sources import them first and then check them out into a different directory (see Section 1.3.1 [Getting the source], page 6).

A.12.1 import options

This standard option is supported by import (see Section A.5 [Common options], page 111, for a complete description):

-m *message*   Use *message* as log information, instead of invoking an editor.

There are the following additional special options.

-b *branch*   See Section 13.6 [Multiple vendor branches], page 101.

-k *subst*   Indicate the keyword expansion mode desired. This setting will apply to all files created during the import, but not to any files that previously existed in the repository. See Section 12.4 [Substitution modes], page 95, for a list of valid '-k' settings.

-I *name*   Specify file names that should be ignored during import. You can use this option repeatedly. To avoid ignoring any files at all (even those ignored by default), specify '-I !'.

name can be a file name pattern of the same type that you can specify in the '.cvsignore' file. See Section C.9 [cvsignore], page 171.

-W *spec*   Specify file names that should be filtered during import. You can use this option repeatedly.

spec can be a file name pattern of the same type that you can specify in the '.cvswrappers' file. See Section C.2 [Wrappers], page 163.

A.12.2 import output

import keeps you informed of its progress by printing a line for each file, preceded by one character indicating the status of the file:

U *file*   The file already exists in the repository and has not been locally modified; a new revision has been created (if necessary).

N *file*   The file is a new file which has been added to the repository.

C *file*   The file already exists in the repository but has been locally modified; you will have to merge the changes.

I *file*   The file is being ignored (see Section C.9 [cvsignore], page 171).

L *file*   The file is a symbolic link; `cvs import` ignores symbolic links. People periodically suggest that this behavior should be changed, but if there is a consensus on what it should be changed to, it doesn't seem to be apparent. (Various options in the 'modules' file can be used to recreate symbolic links on checkout, update, etc.; see Section C.1 [modules], page 159.)

A.12.3 import examples

See Chapter 13 [Tracking sources], page 99, and Section 3.1.1 [From files], page 39.

A.13 log—Print out log information for files

- Synopsis: log [options] [files. . .]
- Requires: repository, working directory.
- Changes: nothing.

Display log information for files. `log` used to call the RCS utility `rlog`. Although this is no longer true in the current sources, this history determines the format of the output and the options, which are not quite in the style of the other CVS commands.

The output includes the location of the RCS file, the *head* revision (the latest revision on the trunk), all symbolic names (tags) and some other things. For each revision, the revision number, the author, the number of lines added/deleted and the log message are printed. All times are displayed in Coordinated Universal Time (UTC). (Other parts of CVS print times in the local timezone).

Warning: `log` uses '-R' in a way that conflicts with the normal use inside CVS (see Section A.5 [Common options], page 111).

A.13.1 log options

By default, `log` prints all information that is available. All other options restrict the output.

-b   Print information about the revisions on the default branch, normally the highest branch on the trunk.

-d *dates*   Print information about revisions with a checkin date/time in the range given by the semicolon-separated list of dates. The date formats accepted are those accepted by the '-D' option to many other CVS commands (see Section A.5 [Common options], page 111). Dates can be combined into ranges as follows:

d1<d2
d2>d1   Select the revisions that were deposited between *d1* and *d2*.

<d
d>   Select all revisions dated *d* or earlier.

d<
>d   Select all revisions dated *d* or later.

d   Select the single, latest revision dated *d* or earlier.

The '>' or '<' characters may be followed by '=' to indicate an inclusive range rather than an exclusive one.

Note that the separator is a semicolon (;).

-h   Print only the name of the RCS file, name of the file in the working directory, head, default branch, access list, locks, symbolic names, and suffix.

-l   Local; run only in current working directory. (Default is to run recursively).

-N   Do not print the list of tags for this file. This option can be very useful when your site uses a lot of tags, so rather than "more"'ing over 3 pages of tag information, the log information is presented without tags at all.

-R   Print only the name of the RCS file.

-r*revisions*   Print information about revisions given in the comma-separated list *revisions* of revisions and ranges. The following table explains the available range formats:

rev1:*rev2*   Revisions *rev1* to *rev2* (which must be on the same branch).

:*rev*   Revisions from the beginning of the branch up to and including *rev*.

rev: Revisions starting with *rev* to the end of the branch containing *rev*.

branch   An argument that is a branch means all revisions on that branch.

branch1 : branch2

> A range of branches means all revisions on the branches in that range.

branch. The latest revision in *branch*.

A bare '-r' with no revisions means the latest revision on the default branch, normally the trunk. There can be no space between the '-r' option and its argument.

-s *states*   Print information about revisions whose state attributes match one of the states given in the comma-separated list *states*.

-t   Print the same as '-h', plus the descriptive text.

-w*logins*   Print information about revisions checked in by users with login names appearing in the comma-separated list *logins*. If *logins* is omitted, the user's login is assumed. There can be no space between the '-w' option and its argument.

log prints the intersection of the revisions selected with the options '-d', '-s', and '-w', intersected with the union of the revisions selected by '-b' and '-r'.

A.13.2 log examples

Contributed examples are gratefully accepted.

A.14 rdiff—'patch' format diffs between releases

- rdiff [-flags] [-V vn] [-r t | -D d [-r t2 | -D d2]] modules...
- Requires: repository.
- Changes: nothing.
- Synonym: patch

Builds a Larry Wall format patch(1) file between two releases, that can be fed directly into the patch program to bring an old release up-to-date with the new release. (This is one of the few CVS commands that operates directly from the repository, and doesn't require a prior checkout.) The diff output is sent to the standard output device.

You can specify (using the standard '-r' and '-D' options) any combination of one or two revisions or dates. If only one revision or date is specified, the patch file reflects differences between that revision or date and the current head revisions in the RCS file.

Note that if the software release affected is contained in more than one directory, then it may be necessary to specify the '-p' option to the `patch` command when patching the old sources, so that `patch` is able to find the files that are located in other directories.

A.14.1 rdiff options

These standard options are supported by `rdiff` (see Section A.5 [Common options], page 111, for a complete description of them):

-D *date*   Use the most recent revision no later than *date.*

-f   If no matching revision is found, retrieve the most recent revision (instead of ignoring the file).

-l   Local; don't descend subdirectories.

-R   Examine directories recursively. This option is on by default.

-r *tag*   Use revision *tag.*

In addition to the above, these options are available:

-c   Use the context diff format. This is the default format.

-s   Create a summary change report instead of a patch. The summary includes information about files that were changed or added between the releases. It is sent to the standard output device. This is useful for finding out, for example, which files have changed between two dates or revisions.

-t   A diff of the top two revisions is sent to the standard output device. This is most useful for seeing what the last change to a file was.

-u   Use the unidiff format for the context diffs. Remember that old versions of the `patch` program can't handle the unidiff format, so if you plan to post this patch to the net you should probably not use '-u'.

-V *vn*   Expand keywords according to the rules current in RCS version *vn* (the expansion format changed with RCS version 5). Note that this option is no longer accepted. CVS will always expand keywords the way that RCS version 5 does.

A.14.2 rdiff examples

Suppose you receive mail from `foo@example.net` asking for an update from release 1.2 to 1.4 of the tc compiler. You have no such patches on hand, but with CVS that can easily be fixed with a command such as this:

```
$ cvs rdiff -c -r F001_2 -r F001_4 tc | \
$$ Mail -s 'The patches you asked for' foo@example.net
```

Suppose you have made release 1.3, and forked a branch called 'R_1_3fix' for bugfixes. 'R_1_3_1' corresponds to release 1.3.1, which was made some time ago. Now, you want to see how much development has been done on the branch. This command can be used:

```
$ cvs patch -s -r R_1_3_1 -r R_1_3fix module-name
cvs rdiff: Diffing module-name
File ChangeLog,v changed from revision 1.52.2.5
to 1.52.2.6
File foo.c,v changed from revision 1.52.2.3
to 1.52.2.4
File bar.h,v changed from revision 1.29.2.1
to 1.2
```

A.15 release—Indicate that a Module is no longer in use

- release [-d] directories...
- Requires: Working directory.
- Changes: Working directory, history log.

This command is meant to safely cancel the effect of 'cvs checkout'. Since CVS doesn't lock files, it isn't strictly necessary to use this command. You can always simply delete your working directory, if you like; but you risk losing changes you may have forgotten, and you leave no trace in the CVS history file (see Section C.11 [history file], page 173) that you've abandoned your checkout.

Use 'cvs release' to avoid these problems. This command checks that no uncommitted changes are present; that you are executing it from immediately above a CVS working directory; and that the repository recorded for your files is the same as the repository defined in the module database.

If all these conditions are true, 'cvs release' leaves a record of its execution (attesting to your intentionally abandoning your checkout) in the CVS history log.

A.15.1 release options

The release command supports one command option:

-d   Delete your working copy of the file if the release succeeds. If this flag is not given your files will remain in your working directory.

> **Warning:** The `release` command deletes all directories and
> files recursively. This has the very serious side-effect that
> any directory that you have created inside your checked-
> out sources, and not added to the repository (using the `add`
> command; see Section 7.1 [Adding files], page 65) will be
> silently deleted—even if it is non-empty!

A.15.2 release output

Before `release` releases your sources it will print a one-line message for
any file that is not up-to-date.

Warning: Any new directories that you have created, but not added to the
CVS directory hierarchy with the `add` command (see Section 7.1 [Adding
files], page 65) will be silently ignored (and deleted, if '`-d`' is specified),
even if they contain files.

U *file*
P *file*
           There exists a newer revision of this file in the repository,
           and you have not modified your local copy of the file ('U'
           and 'P' mean the same thing).

A *file*   The file has been added to your private copy of the sources,
           but has not yet been committed to the repository. If you
           delete your copy of the sources this file will be lost.

R *file*   The file has been removed from your private copy of the
           sources, but has not yet been removed from the repository,
           since you have not yet committed the removal. See Sec-
           tion A.8 [commit], page 123.

M *file*   The file is modified in your working directory. There might
           also be a newer revision inside the repository.

? *file*   *file* is in your working directory, but does not correspond to
           anything in the source repository, and is not in the list of
           files for CVS to ignore (see the description of the '`-I`' option,
           and see Section C.9 [cvsignore], page 171). If you remove
           your working sources, this file will be lost.

A.15.3 release examples

Release the '`tc`' directory, and delete your local working copy of the files.

```
$ cd ..              # You must stand immediately above the
                     # sources when you issue 'cvs release'.
$ cvs release -d tc
You have [0] altered files in this repository.
```

```
Are you sure you want to release (and delete)
directory 'tc': y
$
```

A.16   update—Bring work tree in sync with repository

- update [-AdflPpR] [-d] [-r tag|-D date] files...
- Requires: repository, working directory.
- Changes: working directory.

After you've run checkout to create your private copy of source from the common repository, other developers will continue changing the central source. From time to time, when it is convenient in your development process, you can use the update command from within your working directory to reconcile your work with any revisions applied to the source repository since your last checkout or update.

A.16.1   update options

These standard options are available with update (see Section A.5 [Common options], page 111, for a complete description of them):

-D date   Use the most recent revision no later than *date*. This option is sticky, and implies '-P'. See Section 4.9 [Sticky tags], page 50, for more information on sticky tags/dates.

-f   Only useful with the '-D *date*' or '-r *tag*' flags. If no matching revision is found, retrieve the most recent revision (instead of ignoring the file).

-k *kflag*   Process keywords according to *kflag*. See Chapter 12 [Keyword substitution], page 93. This option is sticky; future updates of this file in this working directory will use the same *kflag*. The status command can be viewed to see the sticky options. See Appendix B [Invoking CVS], page 145, for more information on the status command.

-l   Local; run only in current working directory. See Chapter 6 [Recursive behavior], page 63.

-P   Prune empty directories. See Section 7.5 [Moving directories], page 70.

-p   Pipe files to the standard output.

-R   Update directories recursively (default). See Chapter 6 [Recursive behavior], page 63.

-r rev   Retrieve revision/tag *rev*. This option is sticky, and implies '-P'. See Section 4.9 [Sticky tags], page 50, for more information on sticky tags/dates.

These special options are also available with **update**.

-A   Reset any sticky tags, dates, or '-k' options. See Section 4.9 [Sticky tags], page 50, for more information on sticky tags/dates.

-C   Overwrite locally modified files with clean copies from the repository (the modified file is saved in '.#*file*.*revision*', however).

-d   Create any directories that exist in the repository if they're missing from the working directory. Normally, **update** acts only on directories and files that were already enrolled in your working directory.

         This is useful for updating directories that were created in the repository since the initial checkout; but it has an unfortunate side effect. If you deliberately avoided certain directories in the repository when you created your working directory (either through use of a module name or by listing explicitly the files and directories you wanted on the command line), then updating with '-d' will create those directories, which may not be what you want.

-I *name*   Ignore files whose names match *name* (in your working directory) during the update. You can specify '-I' more than once on the command line to specify several files to ignore. Use '-I !' to avoid ignoring any files at all. See Section C.9 [cvsignore], page 171, for other ways to make CVS ignore some files.

-W*spec*   Specify file names that should be filtered during update. You can use this option repeatedly.

         spec can be a file name pattern of the same type that you can specify in the '.cvswrappers' file. See Section C.2 [Wrappers], page 163.

-j*revision*   With two '-j' options, merge changes from the revision specified with the first '-j' option to the revision specified with the second 'j' option, into the working directory.

         With one '-j' option, merge changes from the ancestor revision to the revision specified with the '-j' option, into the working directory. The ancestor revision is the common ancestor of the revision which the working directory is based on, and the revision specified in the '-j' option.

In addition, each '-j' option can contain an optional date specification which, when used with branches, can limit the chosen revision to one within a specific date. An optional date is specified by adding a colon (:) to the tag: '-j*Symbolic_Tag*:*Date_Specifier*'.

See Chapter 5 [Branching and merging], page 53.

A.16.2 update output

update and checkout keep you informed of their progress by printing a line for each file, preceded by one character indicating the status of the file:

U *file*   The file was brought up to date with respect to the repository. This is done for any file that exists in the repository but not in your source, and for files that you haven't changed but are not the most recent versions available in the repository.

P *file*   Like 'U', but the CVS server sends a patch instead of an entire file. These two things accomplish the same thing.

A *file*   The file has been added to your private copy of the sources, and will be added to the source repository when you run commit on the file. This is a reminder to you that the file needs to be committed.

R *file*   The file has been removed from your private copy of the sources, and will be removed from the source repository when you run commit on the file. This is a reminder to you that the file needs to be committed.

M *file*   The file is modified in your working directory.

'M' can indicate one of two states for a file you're working on: either there were no modifications to the same file in the repository, so that your file remains as you last saw it; or there were modifications in the repository as well as in your copy, but they were merged successfully, without conflict, in your working directory.

CVS will print some messages if it merges your work, and a backup copy of your working file (as it looked before you ran update) will be made. The exact name of that file is printed while update runs.

C *file*   A conflict was detected while trying to merge your changes
                  to *file* with changes from the source repository. *file* (the
                  copy in your working directory) is now the result of at-
                  tempting to merge the two revisions; an unmodified copy
                  of your file is also in your working directory, with the name
                  '.#*file*. *revision*' where *revision* is the revision that your mod-
                  ified file started from. Resolve the conflict as described in
                  Section 10.3 [Conflicts example], page 81. (Note that some
                  systems automatically purge files that begin with '.#' if they
                  have not been accessed for a few days. If you intend to keep
                  a copy of your original file, it is a very good idea to rename
                  it.) Under VMS, the file name starts with '__' rather than
                  '.#'.

? *file*   *file* is in your working directory, but does not correspond to
                  anything in the source repository, and is not in the list of
                  files for CVS to ignore (see the description of the '-I' option,
                  and see Section C.9 [cvsignore], page 171).

Appendix B Quick reference to CVS commands

This appendix describes how to invoke CVS, with references to where each command or feature is described in detail. For other references run the cvs --help command, or see [Index], page 197.

A CVS command looks like:

> cvs [*global_options*]
> > *command* [*command_options*] [*command_args*]

Global options:

--allow-root=*rootdir*

> Specify legal CVSROOT directory (server only) (not in CVS 1.9 and older). See Section 2.9.3.1 [Password authentication server], page 29.

-a

> Authenticate all communication (client only) (not in CVS 1.9 and older). See Section A.4 [Global options], page 109.

-b

> Specify RCS location (CVS 1.9 and older). See Section A.4 [Global options], page 109.

-d *root*

> Specify the CVSROOT. See Chapter 2 [Repository], page 11.

-e *editor*

> Edit messages with *editor*. See Section 1.3.2 [Committing your changes], page 7.

-f

> Do not read the '~/.cvsrc' file. See Section A.4 [Global options], page 109.

-H
--help

> Print a help message. See Section A.4 [Global options], page 109.

-l

> Do not log in '$CVSROOT/CVSROOT/history' file. See Section A.4 [Global options], page 109.

-n

> Do not change any files. See Section A.4 [Global options], page 109.

-Q

> Be really quiet. See Section A.4 [Global options], page 109.

-q

> Be somewhat quiet. See Section A.4 [Global options], page 109.

-r

> Make new working files read-only. See Section A.4 [Global options], page 109.

-s *variable=value*

> Set a user variable. See Section C.12 [Variables], page 173.

-T *tempdir*   Put temporary files in *tempdir*. See Section A.4 [Global options], page 109.

-t   Trace CVS execution. See Section A.4 [Global options], page 109.

-v

--version   Display version and copyright information for CVS.

-w   Make new working files read-write. See Section A.4 [Global options], page 109.

-x   Encrypt all communication (client only). See Section A.4 [Global options], page 109.

-z *gzip-level*
              Set the compression level (client only). See Section A.4 [Global options], page 109.

Keyword expansion modes (see Section 12.4 [Substitution modes], page 95):

    -kkv $Id: file1,v 1.1 1993/12/09 03:21:13 joe Exp $
    -kkvl $Id: file1,v 1.1 1993/12/09 03:21:13 joe Exp harry $
    -kk Id
    -kv   file1,v 1.1 1993/12/09 03:21:13 joe Exp
    -ko   *no expansion*
    -kb   *no expansion, file is binary*

Keywords (see Section 12.1 [Keyword list], page 93):

    $Author: joe $
    $Date: 1993/12/09 03:21:13 $
    $Header: /home/files/file1,v 1.1 1993/12/09 03:21:13 joe
      Exp harry $
    $Id: file1,v 1.1 1993/12/09 03:21:13 joe Exp harry $
    $Locker: harry $
    $Name: snapshot_1_14 $
    $RCSfile: file1,v $
    $Revision: 1.1 $
    $Source: /home/files/file1,v $
    $State: Exp $
    $Log: file1,v $
    Revision 1.1 1993/12/09 03:30:17 joe
    Initial revision

Commands, command options, and command arguments:

add [*options*] [*files*...]

>   Add a new file/directory. See Section 7.1 [Adding files], page 65.

>   -k *kflag*   Set keyword expansion.

>   -m *msg*   Set file description.

admin [*options*] [*files*...]

>   Administration of history files in the repository. See Section A.6 [admin], page 114.

>   -b[*rev*]   Set default branch. See Section 13.3 [Reverting local changes], page 100.

>   -c*string*   Set comment leader.

>   -k*subst*   Set keyword substitution. See Chapter 12 [Keyword substitution], page 93.

>   -l[*rev*]   Lock revision *rev*, or latest revision.

>   -m*rev*:*msg* Replace the log message of revision *rev* with *msg*.

>   -o*range*   Delete revisions from the repository. See Section A.6.1 [admin options], page 115.

>   -q   Run quietly; do not print diagnostics.

>   -s*state*[:*rev*]
>   Set the state.

>   -t   Set file description from standard input.

>   -t*file*   Set file description from *file*.

>   -t-*string*   Set file description to *string*.

>   -u[*rev*]   Unlock revision *rev*, or latest revision.

annotate [*options*] [*files*...]

>   Show last revision where each line was modified. See Section 8.4 [annotate], page 74.

>   -D *date*   Annotate the most recent revision no later than *date*. See Section A.5 [Common options], page 111.

>   -f   Use head revision if tag/date not found. See Section A.5 [Common options], page 111.

>   -l   Local; run only in current working directory. See Chapter 6 [Recursive behavior], page 63.

-R   Operate recursively (default). See Chapter 6
            [Recursive behavior], page 63.

-r *tag*   Annotate revision *tag*. See Section A.5 [Common options], page 111.

checkout [*options*] *modules*...
            Get a copy of the sources. See Section A.7 [checkout], page 120.

-A   Reset any sticky tags/date/options. See Section 4.9 [Sticky tags], page 50 and Chapter 12 [Keyword substitution], page 93.

-c   Output the module database. See Section A.7.1 [checkout options], page 121.

-D *date*   Check out revisions as of *date* (is sticky). See Section A.5 [Common options], page 111.

-d *dir*   Check out into *dir*. See Section A.7.1 [checkout options], page 121.

-f   Use head revision if tag/date not found. See Section A.5 [Common options], page 111.

-j *rev*   Merge in changes. See Section A.7.1 [checkout options], page 121.

-k *kflag*   Use *kflag* keyword expansion. See Section 12.4 [Substitution modes], page 95.

-l   Local; run only in current working directory. See Chapter 6 [Recursive behavior], page 63.

-N   Don't "shorten" module paths if -d specified. See Section A.7.1 [checkout options], page 121.

-n   Do not run module program (if any). See Section A.7.1 [checkout options], page 121.

-P   Prune empty directories. See Section 7.5 [Moving directories], page 70.

-p   Check out files to standard output (avoids stickiness). See Section A.7.1 [checkout options], page 121.

-R   Operate recursively (default). See Chapter 6 [Recursive behavior], page 63.

-r *tag* Checkout revision *tag* (is sticky). See Section A.5 [Common options], page 111.

-s Like -c, but include module status. See Section A.7.1 [checkout options], page 121.

commit [*options*] [*files*...]

 Check changes into the repository. See Section A.8 [commit], page 123.

-F *file* Read log message from *file*. See Section A.8.1 [commit options], page 124.

-f Force the file to be committed; disables recursion. See Section A.8.1 [commit options], page 124.

-l Local; run only in current working directory. See Chapter 6 [Recursive behavior], page 63.

-m *msg* Use *msg* as log message. See Section A.8.1 [commit options], page 124.

-n Do not run module program (if any). See Section A.8.1 [commit options], page 124.

-R Operate recursively (default). See Chapter 6 [Recursive behavior], page 63.

-r *rev* Commit to *rev*. See Section A.8.1 [commit options], page 124.

diff [*options*] [*files*...]

 Show differences between revisions. See Section A.9 [diff], page 126. In addition to the options shown below, accepts a wide variety of options to control output style, for example '-c' for context diffs.

-D *date1* Diff revision for date against working file. See Section A.9.1 [diff options], page 126.

-D *date2* Diff *rev1/date1* against *date2*. See Section A.9.1 [diff options], page 126.

-l Local; run only in current working directory. See Chapter 6 [Recursive behavior], page 63.

-N Include diffs for added and removed files. See Section A.9.1 [diff options], page 126.

-R Operate recursively (default). See Chapter 6 [Recursive behavior], page 63.

-r *rev1* Diff revision for *rev1* against working file. See
     Section A.9.1 [diff options], page 126.

-r *rev2* Diff *rev1*/*date1* against *rev2*. See Section A.9.1
     [diff options], page 126.

edit [*options*] [*files...*]
  Get ready to edit a watched file. See Section 10.6.3 [Editing
  files], page 88.

    -a *actions* Specify actions for temporary watch, where *ac-tions* is edit, unedit, commit, all, or none. See Section 10.6.3 [Editing files], page 88.

    -l   Local; run only in current working directory. See Chapter 6 [Recursive behavior], page 63.

    -R   Operate recursively (default). See Chapter 6 [Recursive behavior], page 63.

editors [*options*] [*files...*]
  See who is editing a watched file. See Section 10.6.4 [Watch
  information], page 89.

    -l   Local; run only in current working directory. See Chapter 6 [Recursive behavior], page 63.

    -R   Operate recursively (default). See Chapter 6 [Recursive behavior], page 63.

export [*options*] *modules...*
  Export files from CVS. See Section A.10 [export], page 128.

    -D *date* Check out revisions as of *date*. See Section A.5 [Common options], page 111.

    -d *dir* Check out into *dir*. See Section A.10.1 [export options], page 129.

    -f   Use head revision if tag/date not found. See Section A.5 [Common options], page 111.

    -k *kflag* Use *kflag* keyword expansion. See Section 12.4 [Substitution modes], page 95.

    -l   Local; run only in current working directory. See Chapter 6 [Recursive behavior], page 63.

    -N   Don't "shorten" module paths if -d specified. See Section A.10.1 [export options], page 129.

-n	Do not run module program (if any). See Section A.10.1 [export options], page 129.
-P	Prune empty directories. See Section 7.5 [Moving directories], page 70.
-R	Operate recursively (default). See Chapter 6 [Recursive behavior], page 63.
-r *tag*	Checkout revision *tag*. See Section A.5 [Common options], page 111.

history [*options*] [*files*...]
Show repository access history. See Section A.11 [history], page 129.

-a	All users (default is self). See Section A.11.1 [history options], page 130.
-b *str*	Back to record with *str* in module/file/repos field. See Section A.11.1 [history options], page 130.
-c	Report on committed (modified) files. See Section A.11.1 [history options], page 130.
-D *date*	Since *date*. See Section A.11.1 [history options], page 130.
-e	Report on all record types. See Section A.11.1 [history options], page 130.
-l	Last modified (committed or modified report). See Section A.11.1 [history options], page 130.
-m *module*	Report on *module* (repeatable). See Section A.11.1 [history options], page 130.
-n *module*	In *module*. See Section A.11.1 [history options], page 130.
-o	Report on checked out modules. See Section A.11.1 [history options], page 130.
-r *rev*	Since revision *rev*. See Section A.11.1 [history options], page 130.
-T	Produce report on all TAGs. See Section A.11.1 [history options], page 130.
-t *tag*	Since tag record placed in history file (by anyone). See Section A.11.1 [history options], page 130.

-u *user*   For user *user* (repeatable). See Section A.11.1
                   [history options], page 130.

-w   Working   directory   must   match.   See
                   Section A.11.1 [history options], page 130.

-x *types*   Report on *types*, one or more of **TOEFWUCGMAR**.
                   See Section A.11.1 [history options], page 130.

-z *zone*   Output for time zone *zone*. See Section A.11.1
                   [history options], page 130.

import [*options*] *repository vendor-tag release-tags*...
         Import files into CVS, using vendor branches. See Sec-
         tion A.12 [import], page 132.

-b *bra*   Import to vendor branch *bra*. See Section 13.6
                   [Multiple vendor branches], page 101.

-d   Use the file's modification time as the time of
                   import. See Section A.12.1 [import options],
                   page 133.

-k *kflag*   Set default keyword substitution mode. See
                   Section A.12.1 [import options], page 133.

-m *msg*   Use *msg* for log message. See Section A.12.1
                   [import options], page 133.

-I *ign*   More files to ignore (! to reset). See Sec-
                   tion A.12.1 [import options], page 133.

-W *spec*   More wrappers. See Section A.12.1 [import op-
                   tions], page 133.

init   Create a CVS repository if it doesn't exist. See Section 2.6
         [Creating a repository], page 25.

log [*options*] [*files*...]
         Print out history information for files. See Section A.13 [log],
         page 134.

-b   Only list revisions on the default branch. See
                   Section A.13.1 [log options], page 134.

-d *dates*   Specify dates (*d1*<*d2* for range, *d* for lat-
                   est before). See Section A.13.1 [log options],
                   page 134.

-h   Only print header. See Section A.13.1 [log op-
                   tions], page 134.

-l	Local; run only in current working directory. See Chapter 6 [Recursive behavior], page 63.
-N	Do not list tags. See Section A.13.1 [log options], page 134.
-R	Only print name of RCS file. See Section A.13.1 [log options], page 134.
-r*revs*	Only list revisions *revs*. See Section A.13.1 [log options], page 134.
-s *states*	Only list revisions with specified states. See Section A.13.1 [log options], page 134.
-t	Only print header and descriptive text. See Section A.13.1 [log options], page 134.
-w*logins*	Only list revisions checked in by specified logins. See Section A.13.1 [log options], page 134.

login   Prompt for password for authenticating server. See Section 2.9.3.2 [Password authentication client], page 32.

logout   Remove stored password for authenticating server. See Section 2.9.3.2 [Password authentication client], page 32.

rdiff [*options*] *modules*...

Show differences between releases. See Section A.14 [rdiff], page 136.

-c	Context diff output format (default). See Section A.14.1 [rdiff options], page 137.
-D *date*	Select revisions based on *date*. See Section A.5 [Common options], page 111.
-f	Use head revision if tag/date not found. See Section A.5 [Common options], page 111.
-l	Local; run only in current working directory. See Chapter 6 [Recursive behavior], page 63.
-R	Operate recursively (default). See Chapter 6 [Recursive behavior], page 63.
-r *rev*	Select revisions based on *rev*. See Section A.5 [Common options], page 111.
-s	Short patch - one liner per file. See Section A.14.1 [rdiff options], page 137.

-t   Top two diffs - last change made to the file. See
                Section A.9.1 [diff options], page 126.

-u   Unidiff output format. See Section A.14.1 [rdiff
                options], page 137.

-V *vers*   Use RCS Version *vers* for keyword expansion
                (obsolete). See Section A.14.1 [rdiff options],
                page 137.

release [*options*] *directory*
        Indicate that a directory is no longer in use. See Section A.15
        [release], page 138.

-d   Delete the given directory. See Section A.15.1
                [release options], page 138.

remove [*options*] [*files*...]
        Remove an entry from the repository. See Section 7.2 [Re-
        moving files], page 66.

-f   Delete the file before removing it. See Sec-
                tion 7.2 [Removing files], page 66.

-l   Local; run only in current working directory.
                See Chapter 6 [Recursive behavior], page 63.

-R   Operate recursively (default). See Chapter 6
                [Recursive behavior], page 63.

rtag [*options*] *tag modules*...
        Add a symbolic tag to a module. See Chapter 4 [Revisions],
        page 43 and Chapter 5 [Branching and merging], page 53.

-a   Clear tag from removed files that would not
                otherwise be tagged. See Section 4.8 [Tagging
                add/remove], page 49.

-b   Create a branch named *tag*. See Chapter 5
                [Branching and merging], page 53.

-D *date*   Tag revisions as of *date*. See Section 4.6 [Tag-
                ging by date/tag], page 48.

-d   Delete *tag*. See Section 4.7 [Modifying tags],
                page 48.

-F   Move *tag* if it already exists. See Section 4.7
                [Modifying tags], page 48.

-f   Force a head revision match if tag/date not found. See Section 4.6 [Tagging by date/tag], page 48.

-l   Local; run only in current working directory. See Chapter 6 [Recursive behavior], page 63.

-n   No execution of tag program. See Section A.5 [Common options], page 111.

-R   Operate recursively (default). See Chapter 6 [Recursive behavior], page 63.

-r *rev*   Tag existing tag *rev*. See Section 4.6 [Tagging by date/tag], page 48.

status [*options*] *files*...

Display status information in a working directory. See Section 10.1 [File status], page 79.

-l   Local; run only in current working directory. See Chapter 6 [Recursive behavior], page 63.

-R   Operate recursively (default). See Chapter 6 [Recursive behavior], page 63.

-v   Include tag information for file. See Section 4.4 [Tags], page 44.

tag [*options*] *tag* [*files*...]

Add a symbolic tag to checked out version of files. See Chapter 4 [Revisions], page 43 and Chapter 5 [Branching and merging], page 53.

-b   Create a branch named *tag*. See Chapter 5 [Branching and merging], page 53.

-c   Check that working files are unmodified. See Section 4.5 [Tagging the working directory], page 47.

-D *date*   Tag revisions as of *date*. See Section 4.6 [Tagging by date/tag], page 48.

-d   Delete *tag*. See Section 4.7 [Modifying tags], page 48.

-F   Move *tag* if it already exists. See Section 4.7 [Modifying tags], page 48.

-f   Force a head revision match if tag/date not
                found. See Section 4.6 [Tagging by date/tag],
                page 48.

-l   Local; run only in current working directory.
                See Chapter 6 [Recursive behavior], page 63.

-R   Operate recursively (default). See Chapter 6
                [Recursive behavior], page 63.

-r *rev*   Tag existing tag *rev*. See Section 4.6 [Tagging
                by date/tag], page 48.

unedit [*options*] [*files*...]
        Undo an edit command. See Section 10.6.3 [Editing files],
        page 88.

-a *actions*   Specify actions for temporary watch, where *ac-
                tions* is **edit**, **unedit**, **commit**, **all**, or **none**.
                See Section 10.6.3 [Editing files], page 88.

-l   Local; run only in current working directory.
                See Chapter 6 [Recursive behavior], page 63.

-R   Operate recursively (default). See Chapter 6
                [Recursive behavior], page 63.

update [*options*] [*files*...]
        Bring work tree in sync with repository. See Section A.16
        [update], page 140.

-A   Reset any sticky tags/date/options. See Sec-
                tion 4.9 [Sticky tags], page 50 and Chapter 12
                [Keyword substitution], page 93.

-C   Overwrite locally modified files with clean
                copies from the repository (the modified file is
                saved in '.#*file*.*revision*', however).

-D *date*   Check out revisions as of *date* (is sticky). See
                Section A.5 [Common options], page 111.

-d   Create directories. See Section A.16.1 [update
                options], page 140.

-f   Use head revision if tag/date not found. See
                Section A.5 [Common options], page 111.

-I *ign*   More files to ignore (! to reset). See Sec-
                tion A.12.1 [import options], page 133.

-j *rev*	Merge in changes. See Section A.16.1 [update options], page 140.
-k *kflag*	Use *kflag* keyword expansion. See Section 12.4 [Substitution modes], page 95.
-l	Local; run only in current working directory. See Chapter 6 [Recursive behavior], page 63.
-P	Prune empty directories. See Section 7.5 [Moving directories], page 70.
-p	Check out files to standard output (avoids stickiness). See Section A.16.1 [update options], page 140.
-R	Operate recursively (default). See Chapter 6 [Recursive behavior], page 63.
-r *tag*	Checkout revision *tag* (is sticky). See Section A.5 [Common options], page 111.
-W *spec*	More wrappers. See Section A.12.1 [import options], page 133.

version

Display the version of CVS being used. If the repository is remote, display both the client and server versions.

watch [on|off|add|remove] [*options*] [*files*...]

on/off: turn on/off read-only checkouts of files. See Section 10.6.1 [Setting a watch], page 86.

add/remove: add or remove notification on actions. See Section 10.6.2 [Getting Notified], page 86.

-a *actions*	Specify actions for temporary watch, where *actions* is **edit**, **unedit**, **commit**, **all**, or **none**. See Section 10.6.3 [Editing files], page 88.
-l	Local; run only in current working directory. See Chapter 6 [Recursive behavior], page 63.
-R	Operate recursively (default). See Chapter 6 [Recursive behavior], page 63.

watchers [*options*] [*files*...]

See who is watching a file. See Section 10.6.4 [Watch information], page 89.

-l	Local; run only in current working directory. See Chapter 6 [Recursive behavior], page 63.

-R   Operate recursively (default). See Chapter 6
            [Recursive behavior], page 63.

Appendix C Reference manual for Administrative files

Inside the repository, in the directory '$CVSROOT/CVSROOT', there are a number of supportive files for CVS. You can use CVS in a limited fashion without any of them, but if they are set up properly they can help make life easier. For a discussion of how to edit them, see Section 2.4 [Intro administrative files], page 23.

The most important of these files is the 'modules' file, which defines the modules inside the repository.

C.1 The modules file

The 'modules' file records your definitions of names for collections of source code. CVS will use these definitions if you use CVS to update the modules file (use normal commands like add, commit, etc).

The 'modules' file may contain blank lines and comments (lines beginning with '#') as well as module definitions. Long lines can be continued on the next line by specifying a backslash ('\') as the last character on the line.

There are three basic types of modules: alias modules, regular modules, and ampersand modules. The difference between them is the way that they map files in the repository to files in the working directory. In all of the following examples, the top-level repository contains a directory called 'first-dir', which contains two files, 'file1' and 'file2', and a directory 'sdir'. 'first-dir/sdir' contains a file 'sfile'.

C.1.1 Alias modules

Alias modules are the simplest kind of module:

mname -a aliases...

> This represents the simplest way of defining a module mname. The '-a' flags the definition as a simple alias: CVS will treat any use of mname (as a command argument) as if the list of names aliases had been specified instead. aliases may contain either other module names or paths. When you use paths in aliases, checkout creates all intermediate directories in the working directory, just as if the path had been specified explicitly in the CVS arguments.

For example, if the modules file contains:

```
amodule -a first-dir
```
then the following two commands are equivalent:
```
$ cvs co amodule
$ cvs co first-dir
```
and they each would provide output such as:
```
cvs checkout: Updating first-dir
U first-dir/file1
U first-dir/file2
cvs checkout: Updating first-dir/sdir
U first-dir/sdir/sfile
```

C.1.2 Regular modules

mname [options] *dir* [*files...*]

> In the simplest case, this form of module definition reduces
> to '*mname dir*'. This defines all the files in directory *dir* as
> module mname. *dir* is a relative path (from `$CVSROOT`) to
> a directory of source in the source repository. In this case,
> on checkout, a single directory called *mname* is created as a
> working directory; no intermediate directory levels are used
> by default, even if *dir* was a path involving several directory
> levels.

For example, if a module is defined by:
```
regmodule first-dir
```
then regmodule will contain the files from first-dir:
```
$ cvs co regmodule
cvs checkout: Updating regmodule
U regmodule/file1
U regmodule/file2
cvs checkout: Updating regmodule/sdir
U regmodule/sdir/sfile
$
```
By explicitly specifying files in the module definition after *dir*, you can
select particular files from directory *dir*. Here is an example:
```
regfiles first-dir/sdir sfile
```
With this definition, getting the regfiles module will create a single working directory 'regfiles' containing the file listed, which comes from a
directory deeper in the CVS source repository:
```
$ cvs co regfiles
U regfiles/sfile
```

```
$
```

C.1.3 Ampersand modules

A module definition can refer to other modules by including '&*module*' in its definition.

    mname [options] &*module*...

Then getting the module creates a subdirectory for each such module, in the directory containing the module. For example, if modules contains

    ampermod &first-dir

then a checkout will create an `ampermod` directory which contains a directory called `first-dir`, which in turns contains all the directories and files which live there. For example, the command

    $ cvs co ampermod

will create the following files:

    ampermod/first-dir/file1
    ampermod/first-dir/file2
    ampermod/first-dir/sdir/sfile

There is one quirk/bug: the messages that CVS prints omit the 'ampermod', and thus do not correctly display the location to which it is checking out the files:

    $ cvs co ampermod
    cvs checkout: Updating first-dir
    U first-dir/file1
    U first-dir/file2
    cvs checkout: Updating first-dir/sdir
    U first-dir/sdir/sfile
    $

Do not rely on this buggy behavior; it may get fixed in a future release of CVS.

C.1.4 Excluding directories

An alias module may exclude particular directories from other modules by using an exclamation mark ('!') before the name of each directory to be excluded.

For example, if the modules file contains:

    exmodule -a !first-dir/sdir first-dir

then checking out the module 'exmodule' will check out everything in 'first-dir' except any files in the subdirectory 'first-dir/sdir'.

C.1.5 Module options

Either regular modules or ampersand modules can contain options, which supply additional information concerning the module.

-d *name*   Name the working directory something other than the module name.

-e *prog*   Specify a program *prog* to run whenever files in a module are exported. *prog* runs with a single argument, the module name.

-i *prog*   Specify a program *prog* to run whenever files in a module are committed. *prog* runs with a single argument, the full pathname of the affected directory in a source repository. The 'commitinfo', 'loginfo', and 'verifymsg' files provide other ways to call a program on commit.

-o *prog*   Specify a program *prog* to run whenever files in a module are checked out. *prog* runs with a single argument, the module name.

-s *status*   Assign a status to the module. When the module file is printed with 'cvs checkout -s' the modules are sorted according to primarily module status, and secondarily according to the module name. This option has no other meaning. You can use this option for several things besides status: for instance, list the person that is responsible for this module.

-t *prog*   Specify a program *prog* to run whenever files in a module are tagged with rtag. *prog* runs with two arguments: the module name and the symbolic tag specified to rtag. It is not run when tag is executed. Generally you will find that taginfo is a better solution (see Section 8.3 [user-defined logging], page 73).

-u *prog*   Specify a program *prog* to run whenever 'cvs update' is executed from the top-level directory of the checked-out module. *prog* runs with a single argument, the full path to the source repository for this module.

You should also see see Section C.1.6 [Module program options], page 163 about how the "program options" programs are run.

C.1.6 How the modules file "program options" programs are run

For checkout, rtag, and export, the program is server-based, and as such the following applies:-

If using remote access methods (pserver, ext, etc.), CVS will execute this program on the server from a temporary directory. The path is searched for this program.

If using "local access" (on a local or remote NFS filesystem, i.e. repository set just to a path), the program will be executed from the newly checked-out tree, if found there, or alternatively searched for in the path if not.

The commit and update programs are locally-based, and are run as follows:-

The program is always run locally. One must re-checkout the tree one is using if these options are updated in the modules administrative file. The file CVS/Checkin.prog contains the value of the option '-i' set in the modules file, and similarly for the file CVS/Update.prog and '-u'. The program is always executed from the top level of the checked-out copy on the client. Again, the program is first searched for in the checked-out copy and then using the path.

The programs are all run after the operation has effectively completed.

C.2 The cvswrappers file

Wrappers refers to a CVS feature which lets you control certain settings based on the name of the file which is being operated on. The settings are '-k' for binary files, and '-m' for nonmergeable text files.

The '-m' option specifies the merge methodology that should be used when a non-binary file is updated. MERGE means the usual CVS behavior: try to merge the files. COPY means that cvs update will refuse to merge files, as it also does for files specified as binary with '-kb' (but if the file is specified as binary, there is no need to specify '-m 'COPY''). CVS will provide the user with the two versions of the files, and require the user using mechanisms outside CVS, to insert any necessary changes. **WARNING:** do not use COPY with CVS 1.9 or earlier–such versions of CVS will copy one version of your file over the other, wiping out the previous contents. The '-m' wrapper option only affects behavior when merging is done on update; it does not affect how files are stored. See Chapter 9 [Binary files], page 75, for more on binary files.

The basic format of the file 'cvswrappers' is:

```
wildcard      [option value] [option value] ...
```

where option is one of

```
    -m       update methodology  value: MERGE or COPY
    -k       keyword expansion   value: expansion mode
```
and value is a single-quote delimited value.

For example, the following command imports a directory, treating files
whose name ends in '.exe' as binary:

```
    cvs import -I ! -W "*.exe -k 'b'" first-dir
       vendortag reltag
```

C.3 The commit support files

The '-i' flag in the 'modules' file can be used to run a certain program
whenever files are committed (see Section C.1 [modules], page 159). The
files described in this section provide other, more flexible, ways to run
programs whenever something is committed.

There are three kind of programs that can be run on commit. They are
specified in files in the repository, as described below. The following table
summarizes the file names and the purpose of the corresponding programs.

'commitinfo'
:   The program is responsible for checking that the commit is
    allowed. If it exits with a non-zero exit status the commit
    will be aborted.

'verifymsg'
:   The specified program is used to evaluate the log message,
    and possibly verify that it contains all required fields. This
    is most useful in combination with the 'rcsinfo' file, which
    can hold a log message template (see Section C.8 [rcsinfo],
    page 170).

'editinfo' The specified program is used to edit the log message, and
    possibly verify that it contains all required fields. This is
    most useful in combination with the 'rcsinfo' file, which
    can hold a log message template (see Section C.8 [rcsinfo],
    page 170). (obsolete)

'loginfo'   The specified program is called when the commit is complete.
    It receives the log message and some additional information
    and can store the log message in a file, or mail it to appro-
    priate persons, or maybe post it to a local newsgroup, or...
    Your imagination is the limit!

C.3.1 The common syntax

The administrative files such as 'commitinfo', 'loginfo', 'rcsinfo', 'verifymsg', etc., all have a common format. The purpose of the files are described later on. The common syntax is described here.

Each line contains the following:

- A regular expression. This is a basic regular expression in the syntax used by GNU emacs.

- A whitespace separator—one or more spaces and/or tabs.

- A file name or command-line template.

Blank lines are ignored. Lines that start with the character '#' are treated as comments. Long lines unfortunately can *not* be broken in two parts in any way.

The first regular expression that matches the current directory name in the repository is used. The rest of the line is used as a file name or command-line as appropriate.

C.4 Commitinfo

The 'commitinfo' file defines programs to execute whenever 'cvs commit' is about to execute. These programs are used for pre-commit checking to verify that the modified, added and removed files are really ready to be committed. This could be used, for instance, to verify that the changed files conform to to your site's standards for coding practice.

As mentioned earlier, each line in the 'commitinfo' file consists of a regular expression and a command-line template. The template can include a program name and any number of arguments you wish to supply to it. The full path to the current source repository is appended to the template, followed by the file names of any files involved in the commit (added, removed, and modified files).

The first line with a regular expression matching the directory within the repository will be used. If the command returns a non-zero exit status the commit will be aborted.

If the repository name does not match any of the regular expressions in this file, the 'DEFAULT' line is used, if it is specified.

All occurrences of the name 'ALL' appearing as a regular expression are used in addition to the first matching regular expression or the name 'DEFAULT'.

Note: when CVS is accessing a remote repository, 'commitinfo' will be run on the *remote* (i.e., server) side, not the client side (see Section 2.9 [Remote repositories], page 26).

C.5 Verifying log messages

Once you have entered a log message, you can evaluate that message to check for specific content, such as a bug ID. Use the 'verifymsg' file to specify a program that is used to verify the log message. This program could be a simple script that checks that the entered message contains the required fields.

The 'verifymsg' file is often most useful together with the 'rcsinfo' file, which can be used to specify a log message template.

Each line in the 'verifymsg' file consists of a regular expression and a command-line template. The template must include a program name, and can include any number of arguments. The full path to the current log message template file is appended to the template.

One thing that should be noted is that the 'ALL' keyword is not supported. If more than one matching line is found, the first one is used. This can be useful for specifying a default verification script in a directory, and then overriding it in a subdirectory.

If the repository name does not match any of the regular expressions in this file, the 'DEFAULT' line is used, if it is specified.

If the verification script exits with a non-zero exit status, the commit is aborted.

Note that the verification script cannot change the log message; it can merely accept it or reject it.

The following is a little silly example of a 'verifymsg' file, together with the corresponding 'rcsinfo' file, the log message template and an verification script. We begin with the log message template. We want to always record a bug-id number on the first line of the log message. The rest of log message is free text. The following template is found in the file '/usr/cvssupport/tc.template'.

```
    BugId:
```

The script '/usr/cvssupport/bugid.verify' is used to evaluate the log message.

```
#!/bin/sh
#
#        bugid.verify filename
#
#  Verify that the log message contains a valid bugid
#  on the first line.
#
if head -1 <$1 |grep '^BugId:[ ]*[0-9][0-9]*$' >/dev/null;
then
```

```
        exit 0
    else
        echo "No BugId found."
        exit 1
    fi
```

The 'verifymsg' file contains this line:

```
    ^tc     /usr/cvssupport/bugid.verify
```

The 'rcsinfo' file contains this line:

```
    ^tc     /usr/cvssupport/tc.template
```

C.6 Editinfo

NOTE: The 'editinfo' feature has been rendered obsolete. To set a default editor for log messages use the EDITOR environment variable (see Appendix D [Environment variables], page 177) or the '-e' global option (see Section A.4 [Global options], page 109). See Section C.5 [verifymsg], page 166, for information on the use of the 'verifymsg' feature for evaluating log messages.

If you want to make sure that all log messages look the same way, you can use the 'editinfo' file to specify a program that is used to edit the log message. This program could be a custom-made editor that always enforces a certain style of the log message, or maybe a simple shell script that calls an editor, and checks that the entered message contains the required fields.

If no matching line is found in the 'editinfo' file, the editor specified in the environment variable $CVSEDITOR is used instead. If that variable is not set, then the environment variable $EDITOR is used instead. If that variable is not set a default will be used. See Section 1.3.2 [Committing your changes], page 7.

The 'editinfo' file is often most useful together with the 'rcsinfo' file, which can be used to specify a log message template.

Each line in the 'editinfo' file consists of a regular expression and a command-line template. The template must include a program name, and can include any number of arguments. The full path to the current log message template file is appended to the template.

One thing that should be noted is that the 'ALL' keyword is not supported. If more than one matching line is found, the first one is used. This can be useful for specifying a default edit script in a module, and then overriding it in a subdirectory.

If the repository name does not match any of the regular expressions in this file, the 'DEFAULT' line is used, if it is specified.

If the edit script exits with a non-zero exit status, the commit is aborted.

Note: when CVS is accessing a remote repository, or when the '-m' or '-F' options to cvs commit are used, 'editinfo' will not be consulted. There is no good workaround for this; use 'verifymsg' instead.

C.6.1 Editinfo example

The following is a little silly example of a 'editinfo' file, together with the corresponding 'rcsinfo' file, the log message template and an editor script. We begin with the log message template. We want to always record a bug-id number on the first line of the log message. The rest of log message is free text. The following template is found in the file '/usr/cvssupport/tc.template'.

```
BugId:
```

The script '/usr/cvssupport/bugid.edit' is used to edit the log message.

```
#!/bin/sh
#
#        bugid.edit filename
#
#   Call $EDITOR on FILENAME, and verify that the
#   resulting file contains a valid bugid on the first
#   line.
if [ "x$EDITOR" = "x" ]; then EDITOR=vi; fi
if [ "x$CVSEDITOR" = "x" ]; then CVSEDITOR=$EDITOR; fi
$CVSEDITOR $1
until head -1|grep '^BugId:[ ]*[0-9][0-9]*$' < $1
do  echo -n  "No BugId found.  Edit again? ([y]/n)"
    read ans
    case ${ans} in
        n*) exit 1;;
    esac
    $CVSEDITOR $1
done
```

The 'editinfo' file contains this line:

```
^tc      /usr/cvssupport/bugid.edit
```

The 'rcsinfo' file contains this line:

```
^tc      /usr/cvssupport/tc.template
```

C.7 Loginfo

The 'loginfo' file is used to control where 'cvs commit' log information is sent. The first entry on a line is a regular expression which is tested against the directory that the change is being made to, relative to the $CVSROOT. If a match is found, then the remainder of the line is a filter program that should expect log information on its standard input.

If the repository name does not match any of the regular expressions in this file, the 'DEFAULT' line is used, if it is specified.

All occurrences of the name 'ALL' appearing as a regular expression are used in addition to the first matching regular expression or 'DEFAULT'.

The first matching regular expression is used.

See Section C.3 [commit files], page 164, for a description of the syntax of the 'loginfo' file.

The user may specify a format string as part of the filter. The string is composed of a '%' followed by a space, or followed by a single format character, or followed by a set of format characters surrounded by '{' and '}' as separators. The format characters are:

s   file name

V   old version number (pre-checkin)

v   new version number (post-checkin)

All other characters that appear in a format string expand to an empty field (commas separating fields are still provided).

For example, some valid format strings are '%', '%s', '%{s}', and '%{sVv}'.

The output will be a string of tokens separated by spaces. For backwards compatibility, the first token will be the repository subdirectory. The rest of the tokens will be comma-delimited lists of the information requested in the format string. For example, if '/u/src/master/yoyodyne/tc' is the repository, '%{sVv}' is the format string, and two files (Makefile, foo.c) were modified, the output might be:

    yoyodyne/tc Makefile,1.3,1.4 foo.c,1.12,1.13

As another example, '%{}' means that only the name of the repository will be generated.

Note: when CVS is accessing a remote repository, 'loginfo' will be run on the *remote* (i.e., server) side, not the client side (see Section 2.9 [Remote repositories], page 26).

C.7.1 Loginfo example

The following 'loginfo' file, together with the tiny shell-script below, appends all log messages to the file '$CVSROOT/CVSROOT/commitlog', and any commits to the administrative files (inside the 'CVSROOT' directory) are also logged in '/usr/adm/cvsroot-log'. Commits to the 'prog1' directory are mailed to ceder.

```
ALL /usr/local/bin/cvs-log $CVSROOT/CVSROOT/commitlog $USER
^CVSROOT /usr/local/bin/cvs-log /usr/adm/cvsroot-log
^prog1 Mail -s %s ceder
```

The shell-script '/usr/local/bin/cvs-log' looks like this:

```
#!/bin/sh
(echo "-------------------------------------------------";
 echo -n $2"   ";
 date;
 echo;
 cat) >> $1
```

C.7.2 Keeping a checked out copy

It is often useful to maintain a directory tree which contains files which correspond to the latest version in the repository. For example, other developers might want to refer to the latest sources without having to check them out, or you might be maintaining a web site with CVS and want every checkin to cause the files used by the web server to be updated.

The way to do this is by having loginfo invoke cvs update. Doing so in the naive way will cause a problem with locks, so the cvs update must be run in the background. Here is an example for unix (this should all be on one line):

```
^cyclic-pages (date; cat; (sleep 2; cd /u/www/local-docs;
  cvs -q update -d) &) >> $CVSROOT/CVSROOT/updatelog 2>&1
```

This will cause checkins to repository directories starting with cyclic-pages to update the checked out tree in '/u/www/local-docs'.

C.8 Rcsinfo

The 'rcsinfo' file can be used to specify a form to edit when filling out the commit log. The 'rcsinfo' file has a syntax similar to the 'verifymsg', 'commitinfo' and 'loginfo' files. See Section C.3.1 [syntax], page 165. Unlike the other files the second part is *not* a command-line template. Instead, the part after the regular expression should be a full pathname to a file containing the log message template.

If the repository name does not match any of the regular expressions in this file, the 'DEFAULT' line is used, if it is specified.

All occurrences of the name 'ALL' appearing as a regular expression are used in addition to the first matching regular expression or 'DEFAULT'.

The log message template will be used as a default log message. If you specify a log message with 'cvs commit -m *message*' or 'cvs commit -f *file*' that log message will override the template.

See Section C.5 [verifymsg], page 166, for an example 'rcsinfo' file.

When CVS is accessing a remote repository, the contents of 'rcsinfo' at the time a directory is first checked out will specify a template which does not then change. If you edit 'rcsinfo' or its templates, you may need to check out a new working directory.

C.9 Ignoring files via cvsignore

There are certain file names that frequently occur inside your working copy, but that you don't want to put under CVS control. Examples are all the object files that you get while you compile your sources. Normally, when you run 'cvs update', it prints a line for each file it encounters that it doesn't know about (see Section A.16.2 [update output], page 142).

CVS has a list of files (or sh(1) file name patterns) that it should ignore while running update, import and release. This list is constructed in the following way.

- The list is initialized to include certain file name patterns: names associated with CVS administration, or with other common source control systems; common names for patch files, object files, archive files, and editor backup files; and other names that are usually artifacts of assorted utilities. Currently, the default list of ignored file name patterns is:

```
RCS       SCCS      CVS        CVS.adm
RCSLOG    cvslog.*
tags      TAGS
.make.state         .nse_depinfo
*~        #*        .#*        ,*        _$*       *$
*.old     *.bak     *.BAK      *.orig    *.rej     .del-*
*.a       *.olb     *.o        *.obj     *.so      *.exe
*.Z       *.elc     *.ln
core
```

- The per-repository list in '$CVSROOT/CVSROOT/cvsignore' is appended to the list, if that file exists.

- The per-user list in '.cvsignore' in your home directory is appended to the list, if it exists.

- Any entries in the environment variable $CVSIGNORE is appended to the list.

- Any '-I' options given to CVS is appended.

- As CVS traverses through your directories, the contents of any '.cvsignore' will be appended to the list. The patterns found in '.cvsignore' are only valid for the directory that contains them, not for any sub-directories.

In any of the 5 places listed above, a single exclamation mark ('!') clears the ignore list. This can be used if you want to store any file which normally is ignored by CVS.

Specifying '-I !' to cvs import will import everything, which is generally what you want to do if you are importing files from a pristine distribution or any other source which is known to not contain any extraneous files. However, looking at the rules above you will see there is a fly in the ointment; if the distribution contains any '.cvsignore' files, then the patterns from those files will be processed even if '-I !' is specified. The only workaround is to remove the '.cvsignore' files in order to do the import. Because this is awkward, in the future '-I !' might be modified to override '.cvsignore' files in each directory.

Note that the syntax of the ignore files consists of a series of lines, each of which contains a space separated list of filenames. This offers no clean way to specify filenames which contain spaces, but you can use a workaround like 'foo?bar' to match a file named 'foo bar' (it also matches 'fooxbar' and the like). Also note that there is currently no way to specify comments.

C.10 The checkoutlist file

It may be helpful to use CVS to maintain your own files in the 'CVSROOT' directory. For example, suppose that you have a script 'logcommit.pl' which you run by including the following line in the 'commitinfo' administrative file:

```
ALL    $CVSROOT/CVSROOT/logcommit.pl
```

To maintain 'logcommit.pl' with CVS you would add the following line to the 'checkoutlist' administrative file:

```
logcommit.pl
```

The format of 'checkoutlist' is one line for each file that you want to maintain using CVS, giving the name of the file.

After setting up 'checkoutlist' in this fashion, the files listed there will function just like CVS's built-in administrative files. For example, when checking in one of the files you should get a message such as:

    cvs commit: Rebuilding administrative file database

and the checked out copy in the 'CVSROOT' directory should be updated. Note that listing 'passwd' (see Section 2.9.3.1 [Password authentication server], page 29) in 'checkoutlist' is not recommended for security reasons.

For information about keeping a checkout out copy in a more general context than the one provided by 'checkoutlist', see Section C.7.2 [Keeping a checked out copy], page 170.

C.11 The history file

The file '$CVSROOT/CVSROOT/history' is used to log information for the history command (see Section A.11 [history], page 129). This file must be created to turn on logging. This is done automatically if the cvs init command is used to set up the repository (see Section 2.6 [Creating a repository], page 25).

The file format of the 'history' file is documented only in comments in the CVS source code, but generally programs should use the cvs history command to access it anyway, in case the format changes with future releases of CVS.

C.12 Expansions in administrative files

Sometimes in writing an administrative file, you might want the file to be able to know various things based on environment CVS is running in. There are several mechanisms to do that.

To find the home directory of the user running CVS (from the HOME environment variable), use '~' followed by '/' or the end of the line. Likewise for the home directory of *user*, use '~user'. These variables are expanded on the server machine, and don't get any reasonable expansion if pserver (see Section 2.9.3 [Password authenticated], page 29) is in use; therefore user variables (see below) may be a better choice to customize behavior based on the user running CVS.

One may want to know about various pieces of information internal to CVS. A CVS internal variable has the syntax ${*variable*}, where *variable* starts with a letter and consists of alphanumeric characters and '_'. If the character following *variable* is a non-alphanumeric character other than '_', the '{' and '}' can be omitted. The CVS internal variables are:

CVSROOT   This is the value of the CVS root in use. See Chapter 2
                      [Repository], page 11, for a description of the various ways
                      to specify this.

RCSBIN   In CVS 1.9.18 and older, this specified the directory where
                      CVS was looking for RCS programs. Because CVS no longer
                      runs RCS programs, specifying this internal variable is now
                      an error.

CVSEDITOR
VISUAL
EDITOR   These all expand to the same value, which is the editor that
                      CVS is using. See Section A.4 [Global options], page 109, for
                      how to specify this.

USER   Username of the user running CVS (on the CVS server ma-
                      chine). When using pserver, this is the user specified in the
                      repository specification which need not be the same as the
                      username the server is running as (see Section 2.9.3.1 [Pass-
                      word authentication server], page 29).

If you want to pass a value to the administrative files which the user who
is running CVS can specify, use a user variable. To expand a user variable,
the administrative file contains ${=*variable*}. To set a user variable, spec-
ify the global option '-s' to CVS, with argument *variable=value*. It may
be particularly useful to specify this option via '.cvsrc' (see Section A.3
[~/.cvsrc], page 108).

For example, if you want the administrative file to refer to a test directory
you might create a user variable TESTDIR. Then if CVS is invoked as

     cvs -s TESTDIR=/work/local/tests

and the administrative file contains sh ${=TESTDIR}/runtests, then that
string is expanded to sh /work/local/tests/runtests.

All other strings containing '$' are reserved; there is no way to quote a
'$' character so that '$' represents itself.

C.13 The CVSROOT/config configuration file

The administrative file 'config' contains various miscellaneous settings
which affect the behavior of CVS. The syntax is slightly different from the
other administrative files. Variables are not expanded. Lines which start
with '#' are considered comments. Other lines consist of a keyword, '=',
and a value. Note that this syntax is very strict. Extraneous spaces or
tabs are not permitted.

Currently defined keywords are:

RCSBIN=*bindir*

> For CVS 1.9.12 through 1.9.18, this setting told CVS to look
> for RCS programs in the *bindir* directory. Current versions of
> CVS do not run RCS programs; for compatibility this setting
> is accepted, but it does nothing.

SystemAuth=*value*

> If *value* is 'yes', then pserver should check for users in the
> system's user database if not found in 'CVSROOT/passwd'.
> If it is 'no', then all pserver users must exist in
> 'CVSROOT/passwd'. The default is 'yes'. For more on
> pserver, see Section 2.9.3 [Password authenticated], page 29.

TopLevelAdmin=*value*

> Modify the 'checkout' command to create a 'CVS' directory
> at the top level of the new working directory, in addition to
> 'CVS' directories created within checked-out directories. The
> default value is 'no'.
>
> This option is useful if you find yourself performing many
> commands at the top level of your working directory, rather
> than in one of the checked out subdirectories. The 'CVS'
> directory created there will mean you don't have to specify
> CVSROOT for each command. It also provides a place for
> the 'CVS/Template' file (see Section 2.3 [Working directory
> storage], page 19).

LockDir=*directory*

> Put CVS lock files in *directory* rather than directly in the
> repository. This is useful if you want to let users read from
> the repository while giving them write access only to *direc-*
> *tory*, not to the repository. You need to create *directory*,
> but CVS will create subdirectories of *directory* as it needs
> them. For information on CVS locks, see Section 10.5 [Con-
> currency], page 84.
>
> Before enabling the LockDir option, make sure that you have
> tracked down and removed any copies of CVS 1.9 or older.
> Such versions neither support LockDir, nor will give an error
> indicating that they don't support it. The result, if this
> is allowed to happen, is that some CVS users will put the
> locks one place, and others will put them another place, and
> therefore the repository could become corrupted. CVS 1.10
> does not support LockDir but it will print a warning if run
> on a repository with LockDir enabled.

LogHistory=*value*

> Control what is logged to the 'CVSROOT/history' file. Default of 'TOFEWGCMAR' (or simply 'all') will log all transactions. Any subset of the default is legal. (For example, to only log transactions that modify the '*,v' files, use 'LogHistory=TMAR'.)

Appendix D All environment variables which affect CVS

This is a complete list of all environment variables that affect CVS.

$CVSIGNORE
>A whitespace-separated list of file name patterns that CVS should ignore. See Section C.9 [cvsignore], page 171.

$CVSWRAPPERS
>A whitespace-separated list of file name patterns that CVS should treat as wrappers. See Section C.2 [Wrappers], page 163.

$CVSREAD
If this is set, checkout and update will try hard to make the files in your working directory read-only. When this is not set, the default behavior is to permit modification of your working files.

$CVSUMASK
Controls permissions of files in the repository. See Section 2.2.2 [File permissions], page 14.

$CVSROOT
Should contain the full pathname to the root of the CVS source repository (where the RCS files are kept). This information must be available to CVS for most commands to execute; if $CVSROOT is not set, or if you wish to override it for one invocation, you can supply it on the command line: 'cvs -d cvsroot cvs_command...' Once you have checked out a working directory, CVS stores the appropriate root (in the file 'CVS/Root'), so normally you only need to worry about this when initially checking out a working directory.

$EDITOR
$CVSEDITOR
$VISUAL
Specifies the program to use for recording log messages during commit. $CVSEDITOR overrides $EDITOR. See Section 1.3.2 [Committing your changes], page 7.

$PATH
If $RCSBIN is not set, and no path is compiled into CVS, it will use $PATH to try to find all programs it uses.

$HOME

$HOMEPATH

$HOMEDRIVE

Used to locate the directory where the '.cvsrc' file, and other such files, are searched. On Unix, CVS just checks for HOME. On Windows NT, the system will set HOMEDRIVE, for example to 'd:' and HOMEPATH, for example to '\joe'. On Windows 95, you'll probably need to set HOMEDRIVE and HOMEPATH yourself.

$CVS_RSH   Specifies the external program which CVS connects with, when :ext: access method is specified. see Section 2.9.2 [Connecting via rsh], page 28.

$CVS_SERVER

Used in client-server mode when accessing a remote repository using RSH. It specifies the name of the program to start on the server side when accessing a remote repository using RSH. The default value is cvs. see Section 2.9.2 [Connecting via rsh], page 28

$CVS_PASSFILE

Used in client-server mode when accessing the cvs login server. Default value is '$HOME/.cvspass'. see Section 2.9.3.2 [Password authentication client], page 32

$CVS_CLIENT_PORT

Used in client-server mode when accessing the server via Kerberos. see Section 2.9.5 [Kerberos authenticated], page 34

$CVS_RCMD_PORT

Used in client-server mode. If set, specifies the port number to be used when accessing the RCMD demon on the server side. (Currently not used for Unix clients).

$CVS_CLIENT_LOG

Used for debugging only in client-server mode. If set, everything sent to the server is logged into '$CVS_CLIENT_LOG.in' and everything sent from the server is logged into '$CVS_CLIENT_LOG.out'.

$CVS_SERVER_SLEEP

Used only for debugging the server side in client-server mode. If set, delays the start of the server child process the specified amount of seconds so that you can attach to it with a debugger.

$CVS_IGNORE_REMOTE_ROOT

For CVS 1.10 and older, setting this variable prevents CVS from overwriting the 'CVS/Root' file when the '-d' global option is specified. Later versions of CVS do not rewrite 'CVS/Root', so CVS_IGNORE_REMOTE_ROOT has no effect.

$COMSPEC   Used under OS/2 only. It specifies the name of the command interpreter and defaults to CMD.EXE.

$TMPDIR
$TMP
$TEMP   Directory in which temporary files are located. The CVS server uses TMPDIR. See Section A.4 [Global options], page 109, for a description of how to specify this. Some parts of CVS will always use '/tmp' (via the tmpnam function provided by the system).

On Windows NT, TMP is used (via the _tempnam function provided by the system).

The patch program which is used by the CVS client uses TMPDIR, and if it is not set, uses '/tmp' (at least with GNU patch 2.1). Note that if your server and client are both running CVS 1.9.10 or later, CVS will not invoke an external patch program.

Appendix E Compatibility between CVS Versions

The repository format is compatible going back to CVS 1.3. But see Section 10.6.5 [Watches Compatibility], page 89, if you have copies of CVS 1.6 or older and you want to use the optional developer communication features.

The working directory format is compatible going back to CVS 1.5. It did change between CVS 1.3 and CVS 1.5. If you run CVS 1.5 or newer on a working directory checked out with CVS 1.3, CVS will convert it, but to go back to CVS 1.3 you need to check out a new working directory with CVS 1.3.

The remote protocol is interoperable going back to CVS 1.5, but no further (1.5 was the first official release with the remote protocol, but some older versions might still be floating around). In many cases you need to upgrade both the client and the server to take advantage of new features and bugfixes, however.

Appendix F Troubleshooting

If you are having trouble with CVS, this appendix may help. If there is a particular error message which you are seeing, then you can look up the message alphabetically. If not, you can look through the section on other problems to see if your problem is mentioned there.

F.1 Partial list of error messages

Here is a partial list of error messages that you may see from CVS. It is not a complete list—CVS is capable of printing many, many error messages, often with parts of them supplied by the operating system, but the intention is to list the common and/or potentially confusing error messages.

The messages are alphabetical, but introductory text such as 'cvs update: ' is not considered in ordering them.

In some cases the list includes messages printed by old versions of CVS (partly because users may not be sure which version of CVS they are using at any particular moment).

cvs *command*: authorization failed: server *host* rejected access

> This is a generic response when trying to connect to a pserver server which chooses not to provide a specific reason for denying authorization. Check that the username and password specified are correct and that the CVSROOT specified is allowed by '--allow-root' in 'inetd.conf'. See Section 2.9.3 [Password authenticated], page 29.

file:*line*: Assertion '*text*' failed

> The exact format of this message may vary depending on your system. It indicates a bug in CVS, which can be handled as described in Appendix H [BUGS], page 195.

cvs *command*: conflict: removed *file* was modified by second party

> This message indicates that you removed a file, and someone else modified it. To resolve the conflict, first run 'cvs add *file*'. If desired, look at the other party's modification to decide whether you still want to remove it. If you don't want to remove it, stop here. If you do want to remove it, proceed with 'cvs remove *file*' and commit your removal.

cannot change permissions on temporary directory
                    Operation not permitted

> This message has been happening in a non-reproducible, occasional way when we run the client/server testsuite, both

on Red Hat Linux 3.0.3 and 4.1. We haven't been able to figure out what causes it, nor is it known whether it is specific
to linux (or even to this particular machine!). If the problem does occur on other unices, 'Operation not permitted'
would be likely to read 'Not owner' or whatever the system
in question uses for the unix EPERM error. If you have any
information to add, please let us know as described in Appendix H [BUGS], page 195. If you experience this error
while using CVS, retrying the operation which produced it
should work fine.

cvs [server aborted]: Cannot check out files into the
repository itself
> The obvious cause for this message (especially for
> non-client/server CVS) is that the CVS root is, for
> example, '/usr/local/cvsroot' and you try to check
> out files when you are in a subdirectory, such as
> '/usr/local/cvsroot/test'. However, there is a more
> subtle cause, which is that the temporary directory on the
> server is set to a subdirectory of the root (which is also not
> allowed). If this is the problem, set the temporary directory
> to somewhere else, for example '/var/tmp'; see TMPDIR in
> Appendix D [Environment variables], page 177, for how to
> set the temporary directory.

cannot open CVS/Entries for reading: No such file or directory
> This generally indicates a CVS internal error, and can be
> handled as with other CVS bugs (see Appendix H [BUGS],
> page 195). Usually there is a workaround—the exact nature
> of which would depend on the situation but which hopefully
> could be figured out.

cvs [init aborted]: cannot open CVS/Root: No such file or
directory
> This message is harmless. Provided it is not accompanied by
> other errors, the operation has completed successfully. This
> message should not occur with current versions of CVS, but
> it is documented here for the benefit of CVS 1.9 and older.

cvs [checkout aborted]: cannot rename file *file* to CVS/,,*file*:
Invalid argument
> This message has been reported as intermittently happening
> with CVS 1.9 on Solaris 2.5. The cause is unknown; if you
> know more about what causes it, let us know as described
> in Appendix H [BUGS], page 195.

`cvs [`*command* `aborted]`: `cannot start server via rcmd`

> This, unfortunately, is a rather nonspecific error message which CVS 1.9 will print if you are running the CVS client and it is having trouble connecting to the server. Current versions of CVS should print a much more specific error message. If you get this message when you didn't mean to run the client at all, you probably forgot to specify `:local:`, as described in Chapter 2 [Repository], page 11.

`ci:` *file*`,v: bad diff output line: Binary files - and` `/tmp/T2a22651 differ`

> CVS 1.9 and older will print this message when trying to check in a binary file if RCS is not correctly installed. Reread the instructions that came with your RCS distribution and the INSTALL file in the CVS distribution. Alternately, upgrade to a current version of CVS, which checks in files itself rather than via RCS.

`cvs checkout: could not check out` *file*

> With CVS 1.9, this can mean that the co program (part of RCS) returned a failure. It should be preceded by another error message, however it has been observed without another error message and the cause is not well-understood. With the current version of CVS, which does not run co, if this message occurs without another error message, it is definitely a CVS bug (see Appendix H [BUGS], page 195).

`cvs [login aborted]: could not find out home directory`

> This means that you need to set the environment variables that CVS uses to locate your home directory. See the discussion of `HOME`, `HOMEDRIVE`, and `HOMEPATH` in Appendix D [Environment variables], page 177.

`cvs update: could not merge revision` *rev* `of` *file*`: No such file or` `directory`

> CVS 1.9 and older will print this message if there was a problem finding the `rcsmerge` program. Make sure that it is in your `PATH`, or upgrade to a current version of CVS, which does not require an external `rcsmerge` program.

`cvs [update aborted]: could not patch` *file*`: No such file or` `directory`

> This means that there was a problem finding the `patch` program. Make sure that it is in your `PATH`. Note that despite appearances the message is *not* referring to whether it can find *file*. If both the client and the server are running a current version of CVS, then there is no need for an external

patch program and you should not see this message. But
if either client or server is running CVS 1.9, then you need
patch.

cvs update: could not patch *file***; will refetch**

This means that for whatever reason the client was unable to
apply a patch that the server sent. The message is nothing
to be concerned about, because inability to apply the patch
only slows things down and has no effect on what CVS does.

dying gasps from *server* **unexpected**

There is a known bug in the server for CVS 1.9.18 and older
which can cause this. For me, this was reproducible if I used
the '-t' global option. It was fixed by Andy Piper's 14 Nov
1997 change to src/filesubr.c, if anyone is curious. If you
see the message, you probably can just retry the operation
which failed, or if you have discovered information concerning its cause, please let us know as described in Appendix H
[BUGS], page 195.

end of file from server (consult above messages if any)

The most common cause for this message is if you are using
an external **rsh** program and it exited with an error. In this
case the **rsh** program should have printed a message, which
will appear before the above message. For more information
on setting up a CVS client and server, see Section 2.9 [Remote
repositories], page 26.

cvs [update aborted]: EOF in key in RCS file *file***,v**
cvs [checkout aborted]: EOF while looking for end of string in
RCS file *file***,v**

This means that there is a syntax error in the given RCS
file. Note that this might be true even if RCS can read the
file OK; CVS does more error checking of errors in the RCS
file. That is why you may see this message when upgrading
from CVS 1.9 to CVS 1.10. The likely cause for the original
corruption is hardware, the operating system, or the like. Of
course, if you find a case in which CVS seems to corrupting
the file, by all means report it, (see Appendix H [BUGS],
page 195). There are quite a few variations of this error
message, depending on exactly where in the RCS file CVS
finds the syntax error.

cvs commit: Executing 'mkmodules'

This means that your repository is set up for a version of
CVS prior to CVS 1.8. When using CVS 1.8 or later, the
above message will be preceded by

>   cvs commit: Rebuilding administrative
>   file database

If you see both messages, the database is being rebuilt twice, which is unnecessary but harmless. If you wish to avoid the duplication, and you have no versions of CVS 1.7 or earlier in use, remove -i mkmodules every place it appears in your modules file. For more information on the modules file, see Section C.1 [modules], page 159.

missing author

Typically this can happen if you created an RCS file with your username set to empty. CVS will, bogusly, create an illegal RCS file with no value for the author field. The solution is to make sure your username is set to a non-empty value and re-create the RCS file.

cvs [checkout aborted]: no such tag *tag*

This message means that CVS isn't familiar with the tag *tag*. Usually this means that you have mistyped a tag name; however there are (relatively obscure) cases in which CVS will require you to try a few other CVS commands involving that tag, before you find one which will cause CVS to update the 'val-tags' file; see discussion of val-tags in Section 2.2.2 [File permissions], page 14. You only need to worry about this once for a given tag; when a tag is listed in 'val-tags', it stays there. Note that using '-f' to not require tag matches does not override this check; see Section A.5 [Common options], page 111.

PANIC administration files missing

This typically means that there is a directory named CVS but it does not contain the administrative files which CVS puts in a CVS directory. If the problem is that you created a CVS directory via some mechanism other than CVS, then the answer is simple, use a name other than CVS. If not, it indicates a CVS bug (see Appendix H [BUGS], page 195).

rcs error: Unknown option: -x,v/

This message will be followed by a usage message for RCS. It means that you have an old version of RCS (probably supplied with your operating system), as well as an old version of CVS. CVS 1.9.18 and earlier only work with RCS version 5 and later; current versions of CVS do not run RCS programs.

cvs [server aborted]: received broken pipe signal

> This message seems to be caused by a hard-to-track-down bug in CVS or the systems it runs on (we don't know—we haven't tracked it down yet!). It seems to happen only after a CVS command has completed, and you should be able to just ignore the message. However, if you have discovered information concerning its cause, please let us know as described in Appendix H [BUGS], page 195.

Too many arguments!

> This message is typically printed by the 'log.pl' script which is in the 'contrib' directory in the CVS source distribution. In some versions of CVS, 'log.pl' has been part of the default CVS installation. The 'log.pl' script gets called from the 'loginfo' administrative file. Check that the arguments passed in 'loginfo' match what your version of 'log.pl' expects. In particular, the 'log.pl' from CVS 1.3 and older expects the logfile as an argument whereas the 'log.pl' from CVS 1.5 and newer expects the logfile to be specified with a '-f' option. Of course, if you don't need 'log.pl' you can just comment it out of 'loginfo'.

cvs [update aborted]: unexpected EOF reading *file*,**v**

> See 'EOF in key in RCS file'.

cvs [login aborted]: unrecognized auth response from *server*

> This message typically means that the server is not set up properly. For example, if 'inetd.conf' points to a nonexistent cvs executable. To debug it further, find the log file which inetd writes ('/var/log/messages' or whatever inetd uses on your system). For details, see Section F.2 [Connection], page 190, and Section 2.9.3.1 [Password authentication server], page 29.

cvs server: cannot open /root/.cvsignore: Permission denied
cvs [server aborted]: can't chdir(/root): Permission denied

> See Section F.2 [Connection], page 190.

cvs commit: Up-to-date check failed for '*file***'**

> This means that someone else has committed a change to that file since the last time that you did a **cvs update**. So before proceeding with your **cvs commit** you need to **cvs update**. CVS will merge the changes that you made and the changes that the other person made. If it does not detect any conflicts it will report 'M *file*' and you are ready to **cvs commit**. If it detects conflicts it will print a message saying

> so, will report 'C *file*', and you need to manually resolve the conflict. For more details on this process see Section 10.3 [Conflicts example], page 81.

Usage: diff3 [-exEX3 [-i | -m] [-L label1 -L label3]] file1 file2 file3   **Only one of [exEX3] allowed**

> This indicates a problem with the installation of diff3 and rcsmerge. Specifically rcsmerge was compiled to look for GNU diff3, but it is finding unix diff3 instead. The exact text of the message will vary depending on the system. The simplest solution is to upgrade to a current version of CVS, which does not rely on external rcsmerge or diff3 programs.

warning: unrecognized response '*text*' from cvs server
> If *text* contains a valid response (such as 'ok') followed by an extra carriage return character (on many systems this will cause the second part of the message to overwrite the first part), then it probably means that you are using the ':ext:' access method with a version of rsh, such as most non-unix rsh versions, which does not by default provide a transparent data stream. In such cases you probably want to try ':server:' instead of ':ext:'. If *text* is something else, this may signify a problem with your CVS server. Double-check your installation against the instructions for setting up the CVS server.

cvs commit: [*time*] waiting for *user*'s lock in *directory*
> This is a normal message, not an error. See Section 10.5 [Concurrency], page 84, for more details.

cvs commit: warning: editor session failed
> This means that the editor which CVS is using exits with a nonzero exit status. Some versions of vi will do this even when there was not a problem editing the file. If so, point the **CVSEDITOR** environment variable to a small script such as:

```
#!/bin/sh
vi $*
exit 0
```

F.2 Trouble making a connection to a CVS server

This section concerns what to do if you are having trouble making a connection to a CVS server. If you are running the CVS command line client running on Windows, first upgrade the client to CVS 1.9.12 or later. The error reporting in earlier versions provided much less information about what the problem was. If the client is non-Windows, CVS 1.9 should be fine.

If the error messages are not sufficient to track down the problem, the next steps depend largely on which access method you are using.

:ext: Try running the rsh program from the command line. For example: "rsh servername cvs -v" should print CVS version information. If this doesn't work, you need to fix it before you can worry about CVS problems.

:server: You don't need a command line rsh program to use this access method, but if you have an rsh program around, it may be useful as a debugging tool. Follow the directions given for :ext:.

:pserver: One good debugging tool is to "telnet servername 2401". After connecting, send any text (for example "foo" followed by return). If CVS is working correctly, it will respond with

            cvs [pserver aborted]: bad auth protocol
            start: foo

            If this fails to work, then make sure inetd is working right. Change the invocation in 'inetd.conf' to run the echo program instead of cvs. For example:

            2401 stream tcp nowait root
            /bin/echo echo hello

            After making that change and instructing inetd to re-read its configuration file, "telnet servername 2401" should show you the text hello and then the server should close the connection. If this doesn't work, you need to fix it before you can worry about CVS problems.

            On AIX systems, the system will often have its own program trying to use port 2401. This is AIX's problem in the sense that port 2401 is registered for use with CVS. I hear that there is an AIX patch available to address this problem.

            Another good debugging tool is the '-d' (debugging) option to inetd. Consult your system documentation for more information.

If you seem to be connecting but get errors like:

```
cvs server: cannot open /root/.cvsignore:
  Permission denied
cvs [server aborted]: can't chdir(/root):
  Permission denied
```

then either you haven't specified '-f' in 'inetd.conf' or your system is setting the HOME environment variable for programs being run by inetd. In the latter case, you can either have inetd run a shell script that unsets HOME and then runs CVS, or you can use **env** to run CVS with a pristine environment.

If you can connect successfully for a while but then can't, you've probably hit inetd's rate limit. (If inetd receives too many requests for the same service in a short period of time, it assumes that something is wrong and temporarily disables the service.) Check your inetd documentation to find out how to adjust the rate limit (some versions of inetd have a single rate limit, others allow you to set the limit for each service separately.)

F.3 Other common problems

Here is a list of problems which do not fit into the above categories. They are in no particular order.

- On Windows, if there is a 30 second or so delay when you run a CVS command, it may mean that you have your home directory set to 'C:/', for example (see HOMEDRIVE and HOMEPATH in Appendix D [Environment variables], page 177). CVS expects the home directory to not end in a slash, for example 'C:' or 'C:\cvs'.

- If you are running CVS 1.9.18 or older, and **cvs update** finds a conflict and tries to merge, as described in Section 10.3 [Conflicts example], page 81, but doesn't tell you there were conflicts, then you may have an old version of RCS. The easiest solution probably is to upgrade to a current version of CVS, which does not rely on external RCS programs.

Appendix G Credits

Roland Pesch, then of Cygnus Support `<roland@wrs.com>` wrote the manual pages which were distributed with CVS 1.3. Much of their text was copied into this manual. He also read an early draft of this manual and contributed many ideas and corrections.

The mailing-list `info-cvs` is sometimes informative. I have included information from postings made by the following persons: David G. Grubbs `<dgg@think.com>`.

Some text has been extracted from the man pages for RCS.

The CVS FAQ by David G. Grubbs has provided useful material. The FAQ is no longer maintained, however, and this manual is about the closest thing there is to a successor (with respect to documenting how to use CVS, at least).

In addition, the following persons have helped by telling me about mistakes I've made:

> Roxanne Brunskill `<rbrunski@datap.ca>`,
>
> Kathy Dyer `<dyer@phoenix.ocf.llnl.gov>`,
>
> Karl Pingle `<pingle@acuson.com>`,
>
> Thomas A Peterson `<tap@src.honeywell.com>`,
>
> Inge Wallin `<ingwa@signum.se>`,
>
> Dirk Koschuetzki `<koschuet@fmi.uni-passau.de>`
>
> and Michael Brown `<brown@wi.extrel.com>`.

The list of contributors here is not comprehensive; for a more complete list of who has contributed to this manual see the file 'doc/ChangeLog' in the CVS source distribution.

Appendix H Dealing with bugs in CVS or this manual

Neither CVS nor this manual is perfect, and they probably never will be. If you are having trouble using CVS, or think you have found a bug, there are a number of things you can do about it. Note that if the manual is unclear, that can be considered a bug in the manual, so these problems are often worth doing something about as well as problems with CVS itself.

- If you want someone to help you and fix bugs that you report, there are companies which will do that for a fee. One such company is:

  ```
  Ximbiot
  3216 Sunnyside Ave.
  Harrisburg, PA 17109, USA

  Email: info@ximbiot.com
  Phone: (717) 579-6168
  Fax: (717) 657-1467
  http://www.ximbiot.com/
  ```

- If you got CVS through a distributor, such as an operating system vendor or a vendor of free software CD-ROMs, you may wish to see whether the distributor provides support.

- If you have the skills and time to do so, you may wish to fix the bug yourself. If you wish to submit your fix for inclusion in future releases of CVS, see the file HACKING in the CVS source distribution. It contains much more information on the process of submitting fixes.

- There may be resources on the net which can help. Two good places to start are:

  ```
  http://www.cvshome.org
  http://www.loria.fr/~molli/cvs-index.html
  ```

  If you are so inspired, increasing the information available on the net is likely to be appreciated. For example, before the standard CVS distribution worked on Windows 95, there was a web page with some explanation and patches for running CVS on Windows 95, and various people helped out by mentioning this page on mailing lists or newsgroups when the subject came up.

- It is also possible to report bugs to bug-cvs. Note that someone may or may not want to do anything with your bug report—if you need a solution consider one of the options mentioned above. People probably do want to hear about bugs which are particularly severe in consequences and/or easy to fix, however. You can also increase your odds by being as clear as possible about the exact nature of the bug and any other relevant information. The way to report bugs is to send email to `bug-cvs@gnu.org`. Note that submissions to bug-cvs may be distributed under the terms of the GNU Public License, so if you don't like this, don't submit them. There is usually no justification for sending mail directly to one of the CVS maintainers rather than to `bug-cvs`; those maintainers who want to hear about such bug reports read `bug-cvs`. Also note that sending a bug report to other mailing lists or newsgroups is *not* a substitute for sending it to `bug-cvs`. It is fine to discuss CVS bugs on whatever forum you prefer, but there are not necessarily any maintainers reading bug reports sent anywhere except `bug-cvs`.

People often ask if there is a list of known bugs or whether a particular bug is a known one. The file BUGS in the CVS source distribution is one list of known bugs, but it doesn't necessarily try to be comprehensive. Perhaps there will never be a comprehensive, detailed list of known bugs.

Index

!

!, in modules file 161

#

#cvs.lock, removing 84
#cvs.lock, technical details 17
#cvs.rfl, and backups 25
#cvs.rfl, removing 84
#cvs.rfl, technical details 17
#cvs.tfl 17
#cvs.wfl, removing 84
#cvs.wfl, technical details 17

&

&, in modules file 161

-

-a, in modules file 159
-d, in modules file 162
-e, in modules file 162, 163
-i, in modules file 162, 163
-j (merging branches) 57
-j (merging branches), and keyword
      substitution 60
-k (keyword substitution) 95
-kk, to avoid conflicts during a merge
      60
-o, in modules file 162, 163
-s, in modules file 162
-t, in modules file 162, 163
-u, in modules file 162, 163

.

.# files 143
.bashrc, setting CVSROOT in 11
.cshrc, setting CVSROOT in 11
.cvsrc file 108
.profile, setting CVSROOT in 11
.tcshrc, setting CVSROOT in 11

/

/usr/local/cvsroot, as example
      repository 11

:

:ext:, setting up 28
:ext:, troubleshooting 190
:fork:, setting up 35
:gserver:, setting up 34
:kserver:, setting up 34
:local:, setting up 11
:pserver:, setting up 32
:pserver:, troubleshooting 190
:server:, setting up 28
:server:, troubleshooting 190

<

<<<<<<< 83

=

======= 83

>

>>>>>>> 83

_

_ files (VMS) 143

A

Abandoning work 88
Access a branch 54
add (subcommand) 65
Adding a tag 45
Adding files 65
Admin (subcommand) 114
Administrative files (intro) 23
Administrative files (reference) .. 159
Administrative files, editing them
      24

Alias modules.................. 159
ALL in commitinfo............. 165
Ampersand modules............ 161
annotate (subcommand)......... 74
Atomic transactions, lack of...... 85
Attic......................... 16
Authenticated client, using...... 32
Authenticating server, setting up
  29
Authentication, stream 109
Author keyword................. 93
Automatically ignored files...... 171
Avoiding editor invocation 113

B

Backing up, repository........... 25
Base directory, in CVS directory.. 23
BASE, as reserved tag name 44
BASE, special tag.............. 114
Baserev file, in CVS directory 23
Baserev.tmp file, in CVS directory
  23
Bill of materials................ 103
Binary files.................... 75
Branch merge example 57
Branch number.............. 43, 55
Branch, accessing 54
Branch, check out.............. 54
Branch, creating a.............. 53
Branch, identifying............. 54
Branch, retrieving.............. 54
Branch, vendor-................ 99
Branches motivation............. 53
Branches, copying changes between
  53
Branches, sticky................ 54
Branching..................... 53
Bringing a file up to date 81
Bugs in this manual or CVS 195
Bugs, reporting 195
Builds......................... 103

C

Changes, copying between branches
  53
Changing a log message 116
Check out a branch 54

Checked out copy, keeping 170
Checkin program............... 162
Checkin.prog file, in CVS directory
  22
Checking commits.............. 165
Checking out source 6
checkout (subcommand)........ 120
Checkout program 162
Checkout, as term for getting ready
  to edit 88
Checkout, example 6
checkoutlist.................... 172
Choosing, reserved or unreserved
  checkouts................... 89
Cleaning up 8
Client/Server Operation 26
co (subcommand) 120
Command reference 145
Command structure............. 107
Comment leader 115
commit (subcommand)......... 123
Commit files................... 164
Commit, when to 91
Commitinfo.................... 165
Committing changes............. 7
Common options............... 111
Common syntax of info files..... 165
Compatibility, between CVS versions
  181
Compression 111, 146
COMSPEC, environment variable
  179
config, in CVSROOT........... 174
Conflict markers 83
Conflict resolution.............. 83
Conflicts (merge example) 82
Contributors (CVS program)...... 3
Contributors (manual).......... 193
Copying a repository 26
Copying changes 53
Correcting a log message 116
Creating a branch.............. 53
Creating a project.............. 39
Creating a repository........... 25
Credits (CVS program).......... 3
Credits (manual)............... 193
CVS 1.6, and watches 89
CVS command structure........ 107
CVS directory, in repository 16

CVS directory, in working directory 19
CVS passwd file 30
CVS, history of 3
CVS, introduction to 3
CVS, versions of 181
CVS/Base directory 23
CVS/Baserev file 23
CVS/Baserev.tmp file 23
CVS/Checkin.prog file 22
CVS/Entries file 20
CVS/Entries.Backup file 22
CVS/Entries.Log file 21
CVS/Entries.Static file 22
CVS/Notify file 22
CVS/Notify.tmp file 23
CVS/Repository file 20
CVS/Root file 12
CVS/Tag file 22
CVS/Template file 23
CVS/Update.prog file 22
CVS_CLIENT_LOG, environment variable 178
CVS_CLIENT_PORT 35
CVS_IGNORE_REMOTE_ROOT, environment variable 178
CVS_PASSFILE, environment variable 32
CVS_RCMD_PORT, environment variable 178
CVS_RSH, environment variable 178
CVS_SERVER, and :fork: 35
CVS_SERVER, environment variable 28
CVS_SERVER_SLEEP, environment variable 178
cvsadmin 115
CVSEDITOR, environment variable 7
CVSEDITOR, internal variable 174
cvsignore (admin file), global 171
CVSIGNORE, environment variable 177
CVSREAD, environment variable 177
CVSREAD, overriding 110
cvsroot 11

CVSROOT (file) 159
CVSROOT, environment variable 11
CVSROOT, internal variable 174
CVSROOT, module name 23
CVSROOT, multiple repositories 24
CVSROOT, overriding 109
CVSROOT, storage of files 18
CVSROOT/config 174
CVSUMASK, environment variable 14
cvswrappers (admin file) 163
CVSWRAPPERS, environment variable 163, 177

D

Date keyword 93
Dates 111
Dead state 16
Decimal revision number 43
DEFAULT in commitinfo 165
DEFAULT in editinfo 167
DEFAULT in verifymsg 166
Defining a module 41
Defining modules (intro) 23
Defining modules (reference manual) 159
Deleting files 66
Deleting revisions 117
Deleting sticky tags 50
Deleting tags 48
Descending directories 63
Device nodes 105
Diff 9
diff (subcommand) 126
Differences, merging 59
Directories, moving 70
Directories, removing 68
Directory, descending 63
Disjoint repositories 24
Distributing log messages 169
driver.c (merge example) 81

E

edit (subcommand)............. 88
editinfo (admin file) 167
Editing administrative files...... 24
Editing the modules file 41
Editor, avoiding invocation of ... 113
EDITOR, environment variable ... 7
EDITOR, internal variable...... 174
EDITOR, overriding 109
Editor, specifying per module ... 167
editors (subcommand).......... 89
emerge 84
Encryption 111
Entries file, in CVS directory..... 20
Entries.Backup file, in CVS directory
.... 22
Entries.Log file, in CVS directory
.... 21
Entries.Static file, in CVS directory
.... 22
Environment variables......... 177
Errors, reporting 195
Example of a work-session 6
Example of merge.............. 81
Example, branch merge.......... 57
Excluding directories, in modules file
.... 161
Exit status, of commitinfo 165
Exit status, of CVS 107
Exit status, of editor 189
Exit status, of taginfo 73
Exit status, of verifymsg....... 166
export (subcommand) 128
Export program............... 162

F

Fetching source 6
File had conflicts on merge....... 80
File locking.................... 79
File permissions, general 14
File permissions, Windows-specific
.... 15
File status.................... 79
Files, moving 68
Files, reference manual 159
Fixing a log message 116
Forcing a tag match........... 112
fork, access method 35

Form for log message 170
Format of CVS commands 107

G

Getting started 6
Getting the source 6
Global cvsignore 171
Global options 109
Group......................... 14
GSSAPI....................... 34
Gzip..................... 111, 146

H

Hard links.................... 105
HEAD, as reserved tag name..... 44
HEAD, special tag 114
Header keyword................ 93
history (subcommand).......... 129
History browsing............... 73
History file 173
History files................... 14
History of CVS 3
HOME, environment variable ... 177
HOMEDRIVE, environment variable
.... 177
HOMEPATH, environment variable
.... 177

I

Id keyword 93
Ident (shell command).......... 94
Identifying a branch 54
Identifying files 93
Ignored files 171
Ignoring files.................. 171
import (subcommand).......... 132
Importing files 39
Importing files, from other version
    control systems 40
Importing modules 99
Index 197
Info files (syntax) 165
Informing others 84
init (subcommand)............. 25
Installed images (VMS)......... 15
Internal variables 173

Introduction to CVS 3
Invoking CVS.................. 145
Isolation...................... 73

J

Join........................... 57

K

Keeping a checked out copy 170
Kerberos, using :gserver:......... 34
Kerberos, using :kserver:......... 34
Kerberos, using kerberized rsh ... 28
Keyword expansion.............. 93
Keyword List 93
Keyword substitution............ 93
Keyword substitution, and merging
        60
Keyword substitution, changing
        modes..................... 95
Kflag........................... 95
kinit 35
Known bugs in this manual or CVS
        196

L

Layout of repository............. 11
Left-hand options 109
Linear development 43
Link, symbolic, importing....... 133
List, mailing list 3
Locally Added 79
Locally Modified 79
Locally Removed................ 80
LockDir, in CVSROOT/config .. 175
Locker keyword 93
Locking files 79
Locks, cvs, and backups 25
Locks, cvs, introduction 84
Locks, cvs, technical details 17
log (subcommand) 134
Log information, saving........ 173
Log keyword 93
Log message entry............... 7
Log message template 170
Log message, correcting........ 116
Log message, verifying.......... 166

Log messages 169
Log messages, editing 167
LogHistory, in CVSROOT/config
        175
Login (subcommand) 32
loginfo (admin file) 169
Logout (subcommand).......... 33

M

Mail, automatic mail on commit .. 84
Mailing list 3
Mailing log messages 169
Main trunk and branches 53
make........................... 103
Many repositories 24
Markers, conflict 83
Merge, an example 81
Merge, branch example 57
Merging........................ 53
Merging a branch 57
Merging a file.................. 81
Merging two revisions 59
Merging, and keyword substitution
        60
mkmodules 186
Modifications, copying between
        branches 53
Module status 162
Module, defining 41
Modules (admin file) 159
Modules file 23
Modules file program options ... 163
Modules file, changing.......... 41
modules.db 19
modules.dir 19
modules.pag 19
Motivation for branches 53
Moving a repository 26
Moving directories 70
Moving files 68
Moving tags 49
Multiple developers 79
Multiple repositories............ 24

N

Name keyword 93
Name, symbolic (tag) 44
Needs Checkout 80
Needs Merge 80
Needs Patch 80
Newsgroups 3
notify (admin file) 87
Notify file, in CVS directory 22
Notify.tmp file, in CVS directory
. . . . 23
Number, branch 43, 55
Number, revision- 43

O

Option defaults 108
Options, global 109
Options, in modules file 162
Outdating revisions 117
Overlap 81
Overriding CVSREAD 110
Overriding CVSROOT 109
Overriding EDITOR 109
Overriding RCSBIN 109
Overriding TMPDIR 109
Overview 3
Ownership, saving in CVS 105

P

Parallel repositories 24
passwd (admin file) 30
Password client, using 32
Password server, setting up 29
PATH, environment variable 177
Per-directory sticky tags/dates . . . 22
Per-module editor 167
Permissions, general 14
Permissions, saving in CVS 105
Permissions, Windows-specific 15
Policy 91
Precommit checking 165
pserver (subcommand) 29
PVCS, importing files from 41

R

RCS history files 14
RCS revision numbers 44
RCS, importing files from 40
RCS-style locking 79
RCSBIN, in CVSROOT/config . . 175
RCSBIN, internal variable 174
RCSBIN, overriding 109
RCSfile keyword 94
rcsinfo (admin file) 170
rdiff (subcommand) 136
Read-only files, and -r 110
Read-only files, and CVSREAD
. . . . 177
Read-only files, and watches 86
Read-only files, in repository 14
Read-only mode 110
Read-only repository access 36
readers (admin file) 36
Recursive (directory descending) . . 63
Reference manual (files) 159
Reference manual for variables . . 177
Reference, commands 145
Regular expression syntax 165
Regular modules 160
release (subcommand) 138
Releases, revisions and versions . . . 43
Releasing your working copy 8
Remote repositories 26
Remove (subcommand) 67
Removing a change 59
Removing directories 68
Removing files 66
Removing tags 48
Removing your working copy 8
Renaming directories 70
Renaming files 68
Renaming tags 49
Replacing a log message 116
Reporting bugs 195
Repositories, multiple 24
Repositories, remote 26
Repository (intro) 11
Repository file, in CVS directory
. . . . 20
Repository, backing up 25
Repository, example 11
Repository, how data is stored . . . 12
Repository, moving 26

Repository, setting up 25
Reserved checkouts 79
Resetting sticky tags 50
Resolving a conflict 83
Restoring old version of removed file
.... 59
Resurrecting old version of dead file
.... 59
Retrieve a branch 54
Retrieving an old revision using tags
.... 46
Reverting to repository version ... 88
Revision keyword 94
Revision management 91
Revision numbers 43
Revision numbers (branches) 55
Revision tree.................... 43
Revision tree, making branches ... 53
Revisions, merging differences
between 59
Revisions, versions and releases ... 43
Right-hand options 111
Root file, in CVS directory 12
rsh 28
rsh replacements (Kerberized, SSH,
&c) 28
rtag (subcommand) 48
rtag, creating a branch using 53

S

Saving space 117
SCCS, importing files from 40
Security, file permissions in
repository 14
Security, GSSAPI 34
Security, kerberos 34
Security, of pserver 33
Security, setuid 15
Server, CVS 26
Server, temporary directories 37
Setgid 15
Setting up a repository 25
Setuid 15
Source keyword 94
Source, getting CVS source 3
Source, getting from CVS 6
Special files.................... 105
Specifying dates 111

Spreading information 84
SSH (rsh replacement) 28
Starting a project with CVS 39
State keyword 94
Status of a file 79
Status of a module 162
Sticky date 50
Sticky tags 50
Sticky tags, resetting 50
Sticky tags/dates, per-directory .. 22
Storing log messages 169
Stream authentication 109
Structure...................... 107
Subdirectories 63
Support, getting CVS support .. 195
Symbolic link, importing........ 133
Symbolic links 105
Symbolic name (tag) 44
Syntax of info files 165
SystemAuth, in CVSROOT/config
.... 175

T

tag (subcommand) 47
Tag file, in CVS directory 22
Tag program................... 162
tag, command, introduction 44
tag, creating a branch using 53
Tag, example 45
Tag, retrieving old revisions 46
Tag, symbolic name 44
taginfo 73
Tags 44
Tags, deleting.................. 48
Tags, moving 49
Tags, renaming 49
Tags, sticky.................... 50
tc, Trivial Compiler (example) 6
Team of developers.............. 79
TEMP, environment variable.... 179
Template file, in CVS directory... 23
Template for log message 170
Temporary directories, and server
.... 37
Temporary files, location of 179
Third-party sources 99
Time.......................... 111
Timezone, in input 111

Timezone, in output 134
TMP, environment variable 179
TMPDIR, environment variable
    179
TMPDIR, overriding 109
TopLevelAdmin, in
    CVSROOT/config 175
Trace 110
Traceability 73
Tracking sources 99
Transactions, atomic, lack of 85
Trivial Compiler (example) 6
Typical repository 11

U

Umask, for repository files 14
Undoing a change 59
unedit (subcommand) 88
Unknown 80
Unreserved checkouts 79
Up-to-date 79
update (subcommand) 140
Update program 162
Update, introduction 81
update, to display file status 80
Update.prog file, in CVS directory
    22
Updating a file 81
User aliases 30
User variables 174
USER, internal variable 174
users (admin file) 87

V

Variables 173
Vendor 99
Vendor branch 99

verifymsg (admin file) 166
Versions, of CVS 181
Versions, revisions and releases ... 43
Viewing differences 9
VISUAL, environment variable 7
VISUAL, internal variable 174

W

watch add (subcommand) 86
watch off (subcommand) 86
watch on (subcommand) 86
watch remove (subcommand) 87
watchers (subcommand) 89
Watches 85
wdiff (import example) 99
Web pages, maintaining with CVS
    170
What (shell command) 94
What branches are good for 53
What is CVS not? 4
What is CVS? 3
When to commit 91
Windows, and permissions 15
Work-session, example of 6
Working copy 79
Working copy, removing 8
Wrappers 163
writers (admin file) 36

X

Ximbiot 195

Z

Zone, time, in input 111
Zone, time, in output 134

Printed in the United States
1001400004B/178-183